THE ULTIMATE

GLOW UP

Guide

THE ULTIMATE
GLOW
UP
Guide

A GUIDE TO SELF GROWTH,
SELF CARE, AND BECOMING
THE BEST VERSION OF YOU

ELICIA GOGUEN

mango
PUBLISHING

CORAL GABLES

Cover & Layout Design: Megan Werner
Cover & Interior Illustrations: Nastia, Vector light Studio,
VudiArts

For permission requests, please contact the publisher at:
Mango Publishing Group
2850 S Douglas Road, 2nd Floor
Coral Gables, FL 33134 USA
info@mango.bz

For special orders, quantity sales, course adoptions and
corporate sales, please email the publisher at sales@mango.
bz. For trade and wholesale sales, please contact Ingram
Publisher Services at customer.service@ingramcontent.com
or +1.800.509.4887.

The Ultimate Glow Up Guide: A Guide to Self Growth,
Self Care, and Becoming the Best Version of You

Library of Congress Cataloging-in-Publication number:
2023945359
ISBN: (pb) 978-1-68481-362-9 (hc) 978-1-68481-363-6
(e) 978-1-68481-364-3
BISAC: SELO23000, SELF-HELP / Personal Growth / Self-Esteem

To the younger version of me

who continued to seek light in her darkest times.

CONTENTS

Introduction   9

PART I—A JOURNEY BACK HOME

Chapter One: Summer Is Coming   16

Chapter Two: Self-Sabotage   28

Chapter Three: Starting the Healing Journey   42

PART II—PROJECT: YOU   57

Chapter Four: Uncovering All the Parts of You   58

Chapter Five: Reparenting Yourself   66

Chapter Six: Uncovering Your Shadow   92

Chapter Seven: Rebuilding Self-Confidence   120

Chapter Eight: Your Deck of Cards   230

About the Author   237

INTRODUCTION

At some point in our lives, we become self-aware. In fact, many of us become *incredibly* self-aware. Incredibly self-aware of who we are, and most importantly, *who we are not*. We start noticing how we look, how we fit into social circles, and how we are compared to those around us. For many, this level of awareness of who we are and who we are not at times becomes incredibly painful. It hurts to see how much we don't fit into the beauty standards that are upheld in society. It hurts to notice that we aren't getting chosen or loved by the people we so desperately want in our lives. It hurts to see that we are nowhere near the person we so desperately want to be, *or think we need to be*. The one who has it all. The one who is beautiful, chosen, happy, confident. The one who has successfully achieved their glow up.

Something that continues to fascinate me is, when humans are in pain, without even realizing, we *always* try to find a way out of that pain. For me, the pain I faced in my teenage years, which many of us face, stemmed from the belief that I was nowhere near the person I thought I needed to be. I learned, in order to get out of that pain, I had to glow up. To transform myself physically into the girl who was plastered all over my Tumblr blog. To learn how to flourish and become someone I was not. Someone who had it all. Someone who was picked. Someone who was wanted. Someone who loved what she saw in the mirror because everyone else loved what they saw as well. And so I set forth on that journey.

I set forth to seek ways in which I was going to get closer to becoming *her*. But on this journey, I was faced with the reality that it wasn't as easy as I thought. Just like you, I found myself stuck in never-ending, unhealthy cycles. Cycles of dieting, falling off healthy habits and routines, depression, continuous self-sabotage, self-hate, and endless confusion as to why I kept failing to complete a journey that was supposed to help me become the person I'd always wanted to be. *What was it that I was missing? And why was this journey so hard?*

In this book, I aim to answer that last question. Not only for you, *but for my younger self.* In the first half of this book, I'll take you through my journey of endless cycles of self-sabotage, perfectionism, and self-hate that led me to uncover the real secrets that no one told me about this pursuit of glowing up into a new version of myself. It is my hope that you will see what you've been missing this whole time.

After deep insights and wisdom that I hope you gain from my own journey, the second half of this book will be dedicated to guiding you on a path to learn how to *really* love yourself, how to *really* understand why you get in your own way and, most importantly, how to get out. How to *really* transform your life and create sustainable change in ways you haven't before. But most of all, my hope is to awaken you. Awaken you to the parts of yourself you never knew you had. Awaken *the part of you* that is a self-healer. So that you can finally come back home, to *you*.

Before going on this incredible journey of writing this book, I decided to take a huge leap of faith into the online world of TikTok, YouTube, and my podcast, *The Glow Up Secrets*, in the hopes of becoming a guide, a best friend, and some might even say, a big sister to women all over the world who are craving something more, seeking something deeper, and quite frankly never giving up on themselves in pursuit of their own self-transformation.

I knew that I couldn't be the only one on a journey of self-transformation who struggled with actually transforming. I knew I wasn't the only one who at one point on their glow-up journey realized that there had to be *something* more than just self-care routines, beauty tips and tricks, and simply staring into the mirror saying "I love you" as a self-love practice. And I was right. There were practices, tips, advice, and quite frankly a *whole journey* much deeper than what was being shown to me on the internet that I had yet to experience when I was a teenager.

Until I did. Until I went through the deepest, most transformative journey I could have ever experienced that led to thousands of beautiful women (and even men) all over the world—all different ages, backgrounds, and life circumstances—tuning into my content on a weekly basis to uncover these truths with me. Now you might ask, why me? What about my tips, my advice, my knowledge makes thousands of people continue to seek guidance? In this book, you will find out.

PART I

A JOURNEY
BACK HOME

CHAPTER ONE

SUMMER IS COMING

It all started with Tumblr

"Long hair and tanned skin" was the name of the blog I created to represent everything I ever wanted to be during high school, but wasn't. Every day after school I would run home to my laptop, open up my Tumblr, and start reblogging countless photos of girls who represented the ultimate "it girl." The one who had my dream body, fashion sense, and stress-free lifestyle. This was my safe space, a place where I felt like anything was possible, a place where I could run away from the reality of my high school experience. One that included feeling awkward and uncomfortable in my own skin, feeling so different from many of the girls who attended my high school who didn't resemble me, from skin tone, hair texture, body type, and even socioeconomic status. I would stay up late into the night escaping real life by consuming and reblogging picture-perfect girls who would be wearing clothes I wished I could fit into, had the faces I wished I resembled, the popularity I wished I had, and the homes I wished I lived in.

I wish I had the same body as her was one of the most dominant thoughts I had as a teenager every time I looked in the mirror, facing the reality that I didn't have the same body type as the girls who rocked Victoria's Secret bikinis on a beach on my Tumblr blog. *Why does my hair have to be so difficult?* was another dominant thought I had as I spent hours brushing through my curly hair, hating it because it didn't look like the effortlessly long, straight hair that they had. *Why does my waist have to be so big?* I would ask myself as I saw the "it girls" at school rocking the most popular size-zero

Hollister shorts. The more time I spent aesthetically curating the Tumblr blog that I was so proud of, the more I felt like I was sitting on the sidelines of a fairy tale movie that someone just so happened to forget to write me in. The more time I spent obsessing over the body I didn't have, the lifestyle I didn't live, and the beauty standard I didn't fit into, the more I hated myself for everything that I was not. *If I just had her body*, I thought, *I'd be able to wear those clothes too. If I just had her beauty*, I thought, *life would be so much easier. If I was just HER, my life would be so much better.*

Preparing for summer was always one of my biggest focuses in my teenage years, as I was always faced with the reality of having to wear shorts, lighter clothing, and bikinis as it got warmer out. I couldn't help but focus on how much I didn't resemble the girls on my Tumblr blog, which always had the ideal summer bodies I felt I needed to have. I figured there had to be a way to fix the most annoying problem that was standing in the way of me experiencing life just like the Tumblr girls: my body. Since I was quite internet savvy at the age of sixteen, I decided to Google "how to get skinny before summer," and of course, millions of six-pack abs and cardio plans were posted online. You know the ones where you start with five sit-ups and work your way to a hundred by the end of the month? Yeah, those ones. I remember the first winter I decided to print one of those programs out and told myself that every day after school, no matter how tired I was, I was going to do it. And I did. Every day after school, I would do sit-ups, arm pumps, and run up and down my apartment building stairs for cardio, all while envisioning the girl I knew I was going to become if I just kept going. After my workouts, I would spend countless hours on the Hollister website browsing their newest spring/summer clothes, praying that one day soon I would be able to fit into these clothes and look exactly how all the other girls looked.

You see, one thing about growing up on the internet is that you have access to just about anything you could ever imagine. Want to lose weight? There are people out there teaching you how to do it their way, for free. Curious to know what caused a random breakout on your face? You bet you'll find your answer...or multiple. The downfall of having access to the internet though, especially when you haven't fully developed your ability to critically think, is being bombarded with whatever society is convincing you that you need to fix all your perceived problems. Weight loss programs, bikini bodies, and Tumblr model culture was in at the time, and one thing I was convinced of was that in order to become the girl on my Tumblr page, I needed to change how I looked. So, when I started Googling "how to get a small waist" or "how to get a thigh gap" and random workout plans on the internet arose, for once in my life I felt like I was being given the key that was going to allow me to become *her*. **Do these thoughts sound familiar to you too? Two things we can take comfort in: we are not alone and there is a lot we can learn from our experiences.**

"Wait, why did I just do that?"

Have you ever done something, knowing it was not in alignment with what you want or who you want to be? It's strange how the mind works. As I started my sixteen-year-old, Google-informed, Tumblr-inspired fitness journey, I couldn't help but imagine just how good summer was going to be because of how skinny I was going to get, which in my head equated to popularity and happiness. Although there were other things I wanted to change about myself, such as learning how to straighten my hair, do my makeup, and copy the girls who made "outfit of the day" YouTube videos, achieving a summer body always felt like the hardest thing I had on my goals list. But very quickly, I started running into a problem that was going to be one of the first-ever encounters with parts of myself I realized I couldn't control. One thing about my sixteen-year-old self was that I absolutely loved donuts, popsicles, Iced Capps, chocolate bars, and really anything that contained endless amounts of processed sugar. But, while being on my Tumblr girl fitness journey, I realized that I couldn't keep eating the way I was and eating boxes of Timbits, Iced Capps, and chocolate every day after school was absolutely going to ruin the chances of me having the summer of my life.

Now, we all know eating a ton of sugar isn't healthy and that all the plain, boring, leafy green foods that our moms always try to get us to eat are deemed "healthy." Realizing the state of my teenage diet, I knew I had a problem I needed to fix. Being an internet kid, and quite frankly the internet being the internet, I found another answer to a problem that was getting in the way of the summer of my life: a diet. At the time, there was a well-known diet called the Atkins diet—you know, one of those standard low-carb fad diets where you eat only certain food groups for X amount of days as you slowly subtract more food until you're only eating salads? In which you inevitably drop weight quickly, until you gain it all back after getting sick of the restrictions? Yeah, that one.

So of course, while feeling as if I found another key to unlock the summer of my dreams, I started following this diet. But after only a few days I started to observe something happening within my mind: continuous thoughts about all my favorite foods. I would be sitting in class and the thought of donuts, Iced Capps, and pizza would consume me more than they ever had before. Every time someone walked into class with anything remotely calorie dense, I couldn't help but think how lucky they were to be able to eat that. There were days where I would come home after school knowing there were chocolate-covered granola bars in the cabinet and completely devoured the entire box, feeling as if someone took over my body. I distinctly remember the first time I ever binged on a food item and I thought, *Wait, why did I just do that?* I really started wondering why I couldn't control myself when I was supposed to be on this diet that I knew would get me to my goals. *Why am I doing this? This is literally going to ruin my whole summer*, I thought. You have probably had a similar confusing experience.

This feeling of confusion with my actions and frustration with myself ran through me every time I found myself consuming foods I knew I shouldn't, until I was able to go to sleep and start fresh the next day. But then it would happen again, and again, and again. The constant cravings, thoughts, and obsession with all of the foods I was no longer able to eat, to the point where a part of me once again took over and went for another binge. It got to the point where these cycles of eating would happen every other day and the more times they happened, the more my inner dialogue got stronger. *How could you? You do realize that summer is around the corner, right? Look at your belly... and your waist. You're nowhere near ready for summer. You're failing. You're never going to be **her.***

You're only ready when you've had enough

Maybe I'll just start on Monday, or maybe I need another diet, or another workout plan? Or maybe... It'll just have to be next year that I become "her." We have probably all said, "Diet starts tomorrow," right? These were the thoughts that followed me all throughout my high school and college years anytime I realized just how much I had fallen off the goals I set forth for myself to become the "it girl." The thing is, throughout my early adolescence, dieting and exercising would work to a certain extent. Until it became too difficult to maintain day in and day out, to the point where I would eventually fall victim to the part of me I was convinced clearly wanted to rebel against the idea of becoming a Tumblr girl. *I say that I want to become the girl on my Tumblr blog, so why can't I do it? Why can't I just glow up?* I ended up drowning myself in self-hate, disgust, and feelings of unworthiness every year.

> **"Now, being young, rooted in low self-worth, and always falling short on my goals, I always had this way of thinking that I wasn't fully ready for life."**

Now, being young, rooted in low self-worth, and always falling short on my goals, I always had this way of thinking that I wasn't fully ready for life. Whether that was not feeling ready to go to the beach with my friends because my body wasn't "bikini ready," or only ever talking to boys through text because I couldn't bear to meet them in real life because I never felt pretty enough. Whatever it was that I always desired to experience in my life, I always had this feeling of unreadiness. The unfortunate part of this is that the more I felt like that, the more susceptible I became to social media fad diets and workout plans that I still believed could fix my issues. I was always convinced I was the issue.

There's no denying that we naturally go through some sort of glow-up as we age, and throughout college I slowly started to grow into my features and learned what looked good on me and what didn't. Since I also had a history of cycling through workouts and diets, my physical body ended up transforming more than I really thought. My body, my face, my style, and my personality did change, and people started to notice. The problem was that I still had the same mindset that started this glow-up journey in the first place. I was stuck at sixteen, thinking I was too physically unattractive to put myself out there and live my life, along with an unhealthy obsession of cycling through diets. And because my body did start to transform and I started getting more attention, it kept me addicted to chasing my end goal, to be the "it girl." I started getting attention from boys, I was able to start dressing more and more like the girls on my Tumblr, I was able to post on social media and get the attention that I saw other girls receiving.

The more I attracted the attention I worked so hard to achieve, I started realizing that this feeling was fleeting. I started to realize after spending hours getting ready to take Instagram photos to post in hopes that the guy I was interested in would like the photo was...draining. I started to notice that I was only happy on the days I went to the gym or when I was perfectly following my diet plan even after achieving "close enough" to the Tumblr girl body. I realized there was this unsustainable level of upkeep of my self-worth and confidence that was entirely dependent on external forces such as men, working out, dieting, and social media popularity.

> **" You see, sometimes you have to do things over and over before you realize that it's not working."**

You see, sometimes you have to do things over and over before you realize that it's not working. The realization that I made in my late teens and early twenties was that no matter what I did to try to change my appearance, I would always find myself unsatisfied with my looks. Eventually I realized that I was stuck with an unhealthy relationship with food, fitness, and self-image. I also realized the type of person I wanted to be perceived as online didn't create the life I thought it would. I thought the attention I would get from boys online or offline because of how hot I looked would make me feel at peace. But the truth is, it didn't. It didn't because the type of attention I was chasing was short lived from people who were also chasing the wrong things, and the happiness I thought I was going to feel about my body never lasted because I was unable to sustain such hard and disciplined fitness and health routines. I wanted more. I wanted to feel happy within my body all the time, whether I had done a workout that day or not. I wanted to stop obsessing over every piece of food I ate on the days that I couldn't eat within the harsh rules of whatever diet I was on at the time. Deep down, I just wanted to feel *free*.

One beautiful thing about growing up and maturing is finally getting to a point where you say, *I'm done*. I'm done with entertaining boys who say they want to be with me but refuse to commit. I'm done with following another fad diet from a fitness fanatic on YouTube who is only pushing this diet for the paycheck. I'm done being my own worst critic. I'm done waking up every day and taking actions that I know won't lead me in the direction of what I want in life. I'm just done. But the downfall of coming to this realization at whatever age you might be is that you are never really taught how to stop. Or better yet, how to feel good about yourself without the short term, unhealthy forms of validation. *How, when I've been getting my external validation from others, do I get it in a healthier way? How, when I've been taught through*

social conditioning and my own self-hate to obsess and pick on my
body, do I stop caring about it? How do I stop becoming my own
worst critic? These are all questions that come up for us at some
point. We initially have no idea how to do things a different way.
We have no idea how we're going to "love ourselves" and stop fad
dieting and looking for crappy male validation. Little did I know,
I would find all the answers in ways I could have never imagined.

Although this was only the start of my journey,
I gained a few pieces of beautiful wisdom throughout
this period of time that I want to share with you.

One: You can't let yourself be influenced by people who are
showcasing their most perfect self online and use them as a
standard to hold yourself to in order for you to be happy and get
the love and attention that you desperately want. You have no
idea what goes on behind closed doors of someone who you think
is the pinnacle of health, wealth, and attraction. Even if you
see yourself as that person, for you to believe that the only way
you deserve to have love, attention, and happiness is if you are
this "it girl" is flawed thinking. There's a level of deservingness
that all humans inherently have, which unfortunately isn't
instilled in us at a young age, but that we must continue to bring
ourselves back to. Because if not, we will never feel "enough."

Two: When you're so focused on one specific goal, you strip so
much precious time away from the present moment where you
can experience true happiness and fulfillment. True fulfillment
will not come when you achieve "the thing;" fulfillment comes

when you decide to be in the present and enjoy that moment **even when** your goal hasn't fully been achieved. Waiting to live your life or to be happy until you attain something strips hours, days, weeks, months, years out of your life. Your life's not meant to just be lived in the future tense, your life is also to be lived right now. So how can you learn to live life for what it is right now? How can you learn to be okay with the "in-between," the present, the "un-conformed version of you"?

Three: Change happens in stages and in this phase of my life, I didn't quite realize that "achieving a thing," such as figuring out how to stop dieting or live a healthy lifestyle, wasn't going to be the answer to all of my problems. But I did come to the realization that what I was doing wasn't working and that I no longer wanted to feel like this. And for those who are on a journey of change and self-development, there may be times where you feel lost because you're realizing what you don't want and what's not working, but you also don't know how you're going to get what you do want, and that's okay. In fact, this is actually a time to practice learning how to be okay with the "in-between" of life. The way I like to look at it now in my life is that I'm slowly closing one door, and walking through a hallway with ten new doors I will eventually get to open and explore. Give yourself grace and time to figure out what that next door will be.

CHAPTER TWO

SELF-SABOTAGE

Growing up on the internet

In the years between high school and college trying to find my way in life, I was diagnosed with an autoimmune disease called ulcerative colitis, which influenced my decision to start learning more about the state of physical and mental health. If you don't know what UC is, it's essentially when a lot of inflammation and ulcers develop in your bowels, leading to uncomfortable IBS-like symptoms such as bloating, irregular or too frequent bathroom trips, and even bleeding that can become incredibly unsafe, and you can end up in the hospital. Naturally being an internet kid, I did *a lot* of Googling. I wanted to know where this came from and more importantly, how to get rid of it. There is nothing more disempowering than being told by your doctor you have a disease that creates uncomfortable symptoms, with no real explanation of what caused it, and how you'll just have to deal with it by being on medication all of your life. Although the medication helped me get through so many periods where I was experiencing flare-ups, I really wanted to know why this happened to my body and most importantly, how I could get healthy again.

I would spend hours on Reddit forums, watching YouTube videos, and searching for books for the answers. What I ended up finding was a never-ending hole of hypotheses as to how one develops autoimmune diseases and, in my case, ulcerative colitis. One of the first things I came across was that on one hand, you can definitely be genetically predisposed to certain types of autoimmune diseases such as the one I had. But many times your predisposition can get triggered and in my case, flare-ups can occur due to poor diet, lack of movement and connection with the outside world, and most importantly, external environmental stressors, many of which might be out of your control.

When I first read that diet could have a huge impact on my symptoms and my potential to heal, I was all in. Since I had been so health-focused in my late teens because of my Tumblr phase, it was easy for me to understand how unhealthy food could have an effect on our health and our bodies' ability to function. But what I wasn't fully aware of at the time was that jumping on a new diet, beyond trying to heal from this disease, allowed me to be back in control.

So I started dieting and fixating once again. Low FODMAP, paleo, low-inflammatory foods, vegan...every "healing" diet under the sun, I tried. I spent insane amounts of money on books, expensive foods, and supplements, and spent every waking day listening to health podcasts. But I quickly ran into the same problem that I had back in high school. I couldn't for the life of me stick to any one diet for more than a week without eating sugar and processed foods that every diet told you to cut out. The worst part of this phase was that I had in my mind that in order to heal, I had to eat extremely clean and healthy. I learned what processed, inorganic, "toxic" foods could do to your body from every health and wellness guru on the internet.

This started to cause an excessive amount of daily stress for me as I was navigating my early twenties. Going out with my friends, working at a banquet hall with massive amounts of delicious food, going on dates, and having enough money to buy expensive food items that fit the diet I was supposed to be following all became too much for me to handle. I became chronically stressed, crushed that I felt like I had no real control over my health and, once again, started self-hating. Hating the fact that I thought I did this to myself. Hating the fact that I continued to mess up by not eating the "right" foods to heal myself. Wishing that I could once again be someone I was currently not.

This is where I started to realize just how much I was stuck. Just how much I absolutely hated myself, just how much my body was calling out for help. On the outside I looked like I had it all together, but inside I was falling apart. I needed help. I needed answers. I couldn't do it anymore. So I searched again. I started looking up why I continued to fall off of diets, why I couldn't stop obsessing over my health and quite frankly, why I hated myself so much when I wasn't being perfect. Once I started this search I was welcomed to another side of the internet, a side where people shared similar stories about their struggles with following fad diets and how they don't really work, or how being exposed to excessive amounts of Photoshopped picture-perfect bodies and faces online fuels one's already low self-esteem. I started to realize that what I was being taught and shown on the internet wasn't actually healing my low self-worth, it was fueling it.

You are rooted in your past

Are there any habits you hold on to because they are a safe space?
After starting to notice that cycling through diets and bouts of self-

hate wasn't actually making me feel good, my question was, *why do I keep doing this?* What about these habits were making me feel safe? You might think this a strange question, but there are always payoffs.

I started to observe after my teen and college years that coming home and indulging in unhealthy food and scrolling on Tumblr felt like my safe place. And quite frankly, I started to realize that all throughout my life I would rather be in my room, watching shows to escape reality with some sort of comfort food. Now the question was, what was I escaping from? Well, what I came to realize was it was a behavior that was keeping me comfortable, but underneath that, it was making me feel safe. Looking back at my childhood, I realized there were a lot of things that created a feeling of being unsafe.

Now there are many reasons we feel unsafe, especially as children, but one of the biggest contributors to my experience with feeling this way was that I was raised by a father who I felt unsafe with. Although I look back and know with my entire heart that his intentions weren't ever to make me feel unsafe, that still became my experience. He was very disciplined, strict, and emotionally distant. When my mom left the house, not only did I feel unsafe through the harsh demands he would place on me, having to grow up around someone like that created a lot of sadness within me. To the point where a lot of my childhood memories are ones of always waiting for my mom to come home to save me from the feeling of sadness and loneliness that I felt when she was away, due to the environment I was in with my father.

You see, as children we experience so many big emotions. When we're upset about not being able to tie our shoes, we cry. When we're hungry but haven't been fed, we get agitated. When we feel that dad is driving too fast on the road, we want to scream out and say, "slow down." Essentially, when we experience anything in life, it triggers some sort of internal feeling like sadness, anger, happiness, etc. Unfortunately, some of us have been raised by caregivers who didn't have the emotional capacity to handle our big emotions and subconsciously or consciously taught us that we shouldn't express our emotions or voice our opinions. We learned that being our most authentic selves might have consequences.

> **"** We will essentially do anything we can in the moment to help us deal with the fear that we are experiencing, and this can be called self-soothing.**"**

The problem is that these **emotions don't go away**. For instance, when we feel that dad is driving too fast, which triggers uncertainty and fear, if we're raised by a father who has taught us that there will be consequences if we speak up, cry, or show any sort of emotions that would be an inconvenience to him, then we won't do it. So, what do we do when we feel afraid and we're not able or don't know how to shout out that we are scared? We might freeze, we might hold in our tears, we might even grab the chocolate bar that's in our backpack to help soothe such an uncomfortable feeling. We will essentially do anything we can in the moment to help us deal with the fear that we are experiencing, and this can be called self-soothing.

For me, the way I learned to regulate my emotions was to simply be as quiet as possible in the presence of my father and as good as possible so that I didn't get yelled at. Another way I learned to make myself feel better was eating candy when I was able to get my hands on it. The problem with becoming a child who was quiet, as good as possible, and hyper-focusing on where the candy was, was that it wasn't fully me. Anytime I did feel fear, anger, or any inkling to be myself, I learned to demonize these emotions as I was never taught that these were okay to have or express. Essentially, I learned to self-soothe the best way I knew how, which at that age was to suppress, ignore, and reject my emotions to keep myself safe.

Your inner child is always there

Our next question might be, why do we still do this in our adult life when we're not even in the same situations anymore? Now that I'm older and educated, I know that if I keep eating candy, pretending to be the "nice girl," and never voicing my opinion will not lead me to a fulfilled life. So why can't I stop? The problem is that when we reach adulthood, we've gotten so used to self-soothing any time that *any* emotion comes up, it's become so automatic. For instance, maybe you're no longer in a car with your father where you feel afraid, but you're now in a situation where you've made a mistake for the first time at your job and you have to face your boss the next morning. Or maybe you're not around your father who told you not to cry when your mom is leaving, but the love of your life just broke up with you and you feel the deep level of loneliness and sadness the same way you did in childhood when your mom left. Different situation yes, but it's the same emotion coming up that you've never learned how to handle.

"We've been subconsciously taught that our survival is on the line if we express certain emotions that our caregivers may not know how to, or don't want to, deal with. "

You see, many of us miss the opportunity in childhood to really learn what it's like to handle and process our emotions in healthy ways. We've never learned how to be comfortable or present with emotions such as fear or loneliness, or even learned how to express ourselves when we need help from others when dealing with these emotions. We've been subconsciously taught that our survival is on the line if we express certain emotions that our caregivers may not know how to, or don't want to, deal with. We can even be rejected by parents or friends for expressing our whole authentic selves. As we grow up and experience emotions, interests, and preferences in environments that aren't conducive to nurturing these unique parts of us, we may even start to feel shame, rejection, and indifference when others around us don't accept us. As we grow up, our choice of self-soothing might lessen as we learn how to process emotions and accept ourselves more as we mature, get into healthier environments, or seek the proper therapeutic health. Sometimes though, our self-soothing might actually get stronger depending on the environment we're in, or we might switch our self-soothing techniques depending on our age or the subconscious realization that our technique is no longer working. For example, maybe you're no longer self-soothing with candy or TV shows, but you're now self-soothing through excessive partying and hook-up culture. Whatever it is, we usually all have some way that we cope.

Coping methods

"Whatever it is, there's a part of us that gets activated and goes to a behavior we've learned from the past, or a behavior that we know will give us short-term, temporary emotional relief."

As I was connecting the dots as a college student, I learned that all the things I had been through in my life and continued to experience could all be grouped under one term: stress. The truth is, from the moment you wake up, you're facing all types of stressors. These external stressors that we all face on different levels stir up emotions within us and, when that happens, we try to soothe ourselves. Escaping into the abyss of social media when we feel indifferent at school. Or spending hours in a Netflix binge session when we've come home from a stressful day at work, or maybe even going to the club and getting black-out drunk on the weekends and indulging in hook-up culture to make ourselves feel wanted.

Whatever it is, there's a part of us that gets activated and goes to a behavior we've learned from the past, or a behavior that we know will give us short-term, temporary emotional relief.

The truth is, we can't get away from emotions and nor should we. Feeling fear, sadness, and discomfort can tell us some very important things about life, such as how safe we are or if we're going in the right direction. And when we're able to tune into and work with our emotions, they can actually help us properly navigate life. Think of it as having your emotional guidance system that was never fully nurtured and developed. When we have an underdeveloped emotional guidance system and we continue to ignore it, it can create a lot of disease within the body mentally and physically over time. Let's say I want to do something new in my life like start a dance class or sit with a new group of girls in class; that will instantly create new emotions within me like fear and uncertainty. If I've not learned that it's safe to do these things, or how to process these emotions when they do show up when trying to do something for the first time, I might start to doubt myself to the point where I'd rather just give up to stay safe. This type of repetitive behavior can be detrimental to not only your mind, but your life by keeping you small.

The thing about stress is that it's not only mental, but it's physical. So not only does our thinking that we're in an unsafe environment or inferior to others drive us to do the quickest most "logical" self-soothing habit that we picked up in childhood such as eating candy; such a habit can create more stress on the body in the form of inflammation and disease. Habits such as dependency on candy, escaping into video games, staying in and not hanging out with friends, being glued to an iPhone screen, starting and stopping restrictive diets, holding in emotions that want to be let out, or excessively drinking can and will eventually affect the health of our bodies. Why? Because our bodies need a balanced diet where we're not constantly spiking our blood sugar with candy throughout the day. Our bodies need a calm mind to sleep, or movement to keep our muscles and joints strong and resilient. Most importantly, our emotions need to be expressed and moved so that we aren't carrying this "emotional baggage" with us throughout our lives and within every relationship we form.

Let's take digestion in my case. Studies have shown that when you're constantly in a state of mental or physical stress, your body can move into a sympathetic nervous system state of fight/flight/freeze, which can have an effect on your body's ability to function at optimal levels for digestion. For me, I was under constant stress as a child, and looking back I experienced digestion issues way before I ever got diagnosed with anything in my early twenties. When you're in a stressful situation, your cortisol and adrenaline can raise very high and when that happens, the energy and blood flow that should be going toward your digestion can slow down. Why? Because your body is utilizing your energy and awareness to make sure you're safe by keeping you alert through the production of cortisol and adrenaline so you can run away, if needed. Your body isn't prioritizing digesting the snack you had before recess because it needs to make sure you have enough energy to fight off whatever it is that you have been conditioned to perceive as a threat. To make matters more difficult, many of us when under stress reach for highly processed, sugar-filled foods, which are the ones that allow for a quick hit of dopamine—which is what makes us feel good in the moment. Since we know that eating overly processed and sugar-filled foods on a daily basis is not ideal for the body to begin with, this starts to tax the body.

> **"After experiencing a stressful situation over and over again, your body that would ideally like a calming environment and a healthy balanced meal to rest and digest, starts to have a hard time functioning at its absolute best."**

After experiencing a stressful situation over and over again, your body that would ideally like a calming environment and a healthy balanced meal to rest and digest, starts to have a hard time functioning at its absolute best. Bowel movements become irregular, nutrients aren't getting digested at the rate they should to give you the vitality you need, hormones such as cortisol and adrenaline are secreting at alarming rates, and the list goes on. Especially when it comes to autoimmune diseases, your body gets to a point where it's often in fight mode and it starts to turn on itself and essentially gets used to creating so much inflammation. In small doses, inflammation can actually be beneficial when fighting off infections and foreign invaders in the body, but if your body is getting signals from the brain that there's a need to continue to create more inflammation, this is where it's no longer helpful. When inflammation becomes chronic, it no longer serves you and instead it can hurt you, creating physical reactions like skin issues, gut issues, and bowel issues. When our bodies start to go into overdrive and inflammation starts to occur, it's like our bodies are throwing up huge red flags calling out for help.

Becoming your own healer

When I first recognized the ways I was dealing with stress and how that was negatively impacting my life and health, I was angry at myself for the habits I picked up and, honestly, my entire life circumstance for even triggering me into such fight or flight mode. But when I discovered that the self-soothing habits I was doing were simply ways I was trying to handle stress without realizing, it was like a light bulb moment. All this time, I had been in survival mode. All this time, I was looking for safety. For the first time ever, I no longer looked at my behaviors that always ended up halting my progress as sabotage. I was in survival mode, and my body was calling out for help.

Looking back, there were so many signs of my body calling out for help, and even though I wasn't aware *why* my body was calling out for help, I knew that it was, but I didn't listen. **Have you ever intuitively known when something was off, but you consciously decided to ignore it?** Like when your stomach is bloated after every meal and you notice the discomfort, but once it's gone away, you forget it even happened until the next time it does? Or every time after you drink, you feel incredibly depressed and physically hungover the next day, but decide to do it again next weekend, disregarding how bad you felt the week before? If you listen closely, your body speaks to you in more ways than you could even imagine.

When you're in pain or discomfort, ask yourself:

+ What occurred before I started feeling this way?

+ Did I eat something?

+ Was I under a lot of mental stress?

+ Did I spend a lot of time with people whom deep down I know aren't healthy influences in my life?

+ What triggered my body to speak out like this?

Now it might be an accumulation of many things, over the years, but by slowly trying to connect dots and learning to become the person who knows you and your body *best* is a critical part of transforming your life. More on that later.

CHAPTER THREE

STARTING THE HEALING JOURNEY

Making the commitment

Connecting the dots to what's really going on with you is an amazing stepping stone, but it's really only the first step in your healing process. There's still work to be done. Healing, like anything else, takes time. It takes you finding the right people, the right medication if necessary, and the right environment so that you can not only heal but grow and prosper. Once I started experiencing chronic pain in my hands, I knew that my journey wasn't over.

What is this pain in my hands? Is it carpal tunnel? Is it nerve damage? What the hell is it and when will it be over? This last thought was the recurring question I had for a solid two years when I realized I was dealing with nerve pain in both hands, which felt like pins and needles, inflammation, and restriction. The confusing part about this mysterious nerve pain was that I was too young to have something like carpal tunnel in my twenties; I also didn't have a job where I was doing repetitive computer work. When I started feeling this mysterious hand pain, I first tried to ignore it, until it took over my life, my job, and my daily routines. I couldn't use my computer or phone, brush my hair, or make myself breakfast without feeling pain and, worst of all, I didn't know how to get out of it.

After months and months of working with doctors to rule out what it was, I started to become increasingly frustrated and scared. *Is my life over? Is my future over? If I can't use my hands... Then what do I have?* This was an incredibly stressful time for me as I was still trying to heal from the complicated relationship I had with myself, along with trying to keep my head afloat with my finances, while struggling with an unhealthy relationship with my mother as she struggled with her addictions. But as a seemingly healthy twenty-four-year-old women, doctors could not figure out why I had this pain and why it became chronic. Doctors took inflammation blood tests, nerve conduction tests, gave me cortisone shots in my wrists, took MRIs, put me on pain management ketamine injections, tried physiotherapy, chiropractors, and acupuncture, and I was even sent to a hand surgeon who was about to operate on my hands until he felt in his gut that it wasn't carpal tunnel.

As I was waiting for an answer that didn't seem to want to come from the doctors, I realized that the mental stress I was experiencing during this period was getting worse and aside from trying to physically heal, I needed to support my mental health the best way I could. After taking a leave of absence, I decided my mental health needed to be my focus. All I knew was that I just wanted to be out of pain, and although I had no idea how I was going to get out of it, I did know that if I kept stressing, obsessing, and focusing on it, I would definitely never get out of it.

> **" I realized I could still have a healthy level of control over my life by doing what I *could* in that moment, instead of focusing on what I couldn't do."**

So I told myself, and my mother did as well, to trust that *someone, somewhere* would have an answer and until then, simply take care of myself in the meanwhile. See, that was something I struggled with...waiting. I was so used to having control over my life, whether that be controlling what I ate, deciding what time I was going to clean my apartment or do my errands, when to get up to go to work, etc. And I felt like I lost control of my entire life with no light of day, until I started to change my perspective. I realized I could still have a healthy level of control over my life by doing what I *could* in that moment, instead of focusing on what I couldn't do. Making the commitment to being patient and learning how to aid myself as I got answers was a form of control, and so I committed.

Doing the thing

Instead of watching people on YouTube live their best lives, which would trigger me to think about the life that was slipping away from me, I decided to start using my time for things that enriched me. I naturally started watching university lectures on psychology, sociology, geography, biology... Things I knew I really wanted to get a better understanding of that I didn't ever find the time for. I started working out the best way I could by learning movements that didn't involve using too much of my hands, along with going on hour-long walks around my neighborhood while listening to podcasts or music that got me in a positive mindset. I started asking my mom to cook me healthier foods instead of making the excuse that I couldn't eat healthy food because I couldn't cook and therefore had to opt for packaged foods. I started sleeping regularly and overall taking care of myself like I would if I wasn't in pain. I started speaking more positively about my situation to my mom, friends, and family around me and having more trust and belief that eventually something would change.

One day, when I was stretching on my floor, doing hand exercises from my physio (which I was subconsciously convinced didn't really do anything but give me a placebo effect), a podcast episode started to play in my queue with a psychologist being interviewed about mental health and its link to chronic pain. Prior to this I was listening to a lot of mental health and self-improvement podcasts, and I had done extensive research on carpal tunnel and hand pain but had exhausted all the options. But something about this podcast episode intrigued me, so I decided to keep listening.

It was essentially a podcast where this man was interviewing a research psychologist about how mental stress can affect the physical body. How your pain systems that are wired through your nerve pathways can be miscommunicating and sending the wrong signals or heightened signals to parts of your body in the form of pain. How, when in a state of stress for long periods of time, your pain tolerance is much higher. I won't go into the science here but essentially, she opened the door to the realization that mental and emotional stress can affect the way the body is operating and feels. Once I heard that, I realized I needed to look into this further, so I searched on the internet for people talking about the mind-body connection and how chronic illness has a mental health component. How your biology, psychology, and social environment all play a role in your current state of physical health. The more I researched, the more I learned about how a nervous system state of fight/flight/freeze, when stuck, can create a host of not just diseases—which at that point I believed was the reason for my UC—but also pain in the body even when there isn't anything structurally wrong. The medical term for this is called psychosomatic pain, which is when someone may experience excessive levels of mental stress that can manifest physically in your muscular-skeletal system. Sometimes, and in my case, psychosomatic pain becomes a mystery because you feel the pain, but there's nothing to be found "wrong" structurally.

The game changer

At this point, I started to believe this was true because I had exhausted every medical option. I saw the charts and tests, I took the medication, I did the exercises and, most importantly, I saw the confusion on every medical practitioner's face. Another thing I started to notice was that when I was mentally stressed by thinking of my future, or the frustration I felt when I wanted to cook my own food but couldn't, my pain always seemed to be heighted. But alternatively, when I felt like I was getting answers, taking new medication, or going for a new procedure, my hands always felt much less painful. I came to realize that my mental state of stress or relaxation had a direct effect on the physical feeling in my hands.

This is where I started reading up on the importance of nervous system regulation. This is essentially when you practice calming your mind and learning how to respond differently to stressors in your life, which helps to regulate your nervous system and, in turn, can reduce pain. I'd always heard of the benefits of meditating and being present, etc., but I didn't realize the power it could have on my body. I was never one to meditate because I could never stay focused. **This is one of the most common things said about meditation, so I'm sure you've experienced it too.** Trying to reintegrate it back into my life as a method to help me with my hand pain was something I quite frankly couldn't do, because the moment my eyes opened in the morning I was already thinking about my pain. My focus on my pain was simply too strong to sit in silence, until I came across this YouTube channel that had a host of *guided* meditations specifically for chronic pain. Considering the amount of time I had on my hands, I figured I'd try it out.

This is where the game changed for me. For the first time, I learned how to experience my chronic pain differently. These meditations guided me in a way where I no longer had to be afraid of the pain or stress about the pain. The woman guiding me would ask questions like, "What would it be like if you just sat with the pain right now?" and furthermore, guided me to take my focus off the pain and onto other parts of my body that were out of pain. Sometimes, she would even speak healing, positive affirmations throughout the meditation. After fifteen to twenty minutes of being guided by someone on the internet, I realized my body felt calmer than it had felt before I started, my mental state was clear, I felt more grateful and less scared, but, most importantly, I was in less pain.

"I couldn't believe that I wasn't alone."

How could I replicate this? How could I get to a point where my pain is fully gone? I continued my search into the world of mind-body

STARTING THE HEALING JOURNEY   ♦   49

connection, realizing how powerful your state of mind can be on your body. I found Dr. Sarno, a professor of rehabilitation and researcher on psychosomatic pain along with stories online of many people who had back pain, hand pain, and all sorts of physical ailments who experienced the same type of psychosomatic pain I did. The kind of ailments that doctors usually had no answers for. I couldn't believe that I wasn't alone. On my search I ended up finding a woman named Nicole Sachs who worked alongside Dr. Sarno. She had created a whole podcast dedicated to educating people on the mind-body connection and the importance of looking at how your nervous system, which was first formed in childhood through big or small trauma, is essentially in chronic fight/flight/freeze mode and wants you to listen.

Most importantly, what I learned through my search was that when you have learned over the years to suppress emotions like sadness, fear, or anger, they don't just disappear into thin air. In fact, you actually hold onto your emotions to a point where they start to affect your physical body. You know this to be true when someone crosses a boundary with you at work, and because of the hierarchy, you tell yourself to hold onto that feeling of anger or frustration. Stop and think about what happens when you feel that emotion: your heart starts racing, your hands get sweaty, your mind can't stop thinking about the situation and it might even take a long time for you to come down from that feeling. There was essentially an external force that triggered your awareness to a point where your body started to react.

Now what happens when you've never learned how to let it all out? What happens after years and years of being in an environment where you were taught that you shouldn't let out your emotions or that if you do, it's a threat to your survival? What happens if the only way you've ever learned how to cope with your emotions is through unhealthy behaviors? Well, what I learned is that your body can only handle being out of homeostasis for a certain amount of time before it starts to break down. **You have probably experienced something like this at least once in your life when, because of what's happening in your mind, you physically become ill.** Thinking back to when I was a child and my nervous system was primed to be in high alert, it would have been hard for my body to be in balance and function at its prime when under so much stress, and the same was true even as an adult. My nervous system was in overdrive and so were my pain signals. I realized it wasn't that I was making up the fact that I felt pain, but it wasn't the full picture. My body was trying to show me that something internally wasn't functioning properly, but I was simply looking in the wrong places.

The next level

" When you release emotions that you've been carrying for a long time, it can free up the space in your mind and even in your body to heal."

How can you reset your nervous system to its healthy state, called the parasympathetic state of rest and digest? What Nicole Sachs had taught me was the opposite of what I'd been taught to do all my life, which was to release my emotions. When you release emotions that you've been carrying for a long time, it can free up the space in your mind and even in your body to heal. My Somatic therapist also taught me the same. She essentially taught me my nervous system was the thing I had been ignoring that needed my attention. After a full year of doctors giving me no answers and educating myself on trauma, the nervous system, and pain regulation, I decided I would dive in further. Dive into becoming the person who believed she could find her way out of pain through what some people call "alternative healing practices."

So I started to journal. I journaled every emotion, every thought, everything that I was feeling. Not just from the present moment, but also from the past. This included the anger I felt toward my father who made me so afraid to be around him, for the relationship we never had, and for the fact that he was no longer on this earth anymore. Anger toward my mother for not protecting me more, anger toward her for missing my early adult years due to substance abuse. Anger toward all the relationships that didn't work out because these men weren't "ready," and anger toward myself for all the stupid mistakes I told myself I made based out of a need for survival. All the sadness I felt for the relationships I lost, the sadness for my inner child that had been hurting all these years. All the jealousy I felt toward people who were living out my dream life as I sat there every day in pain. Everything I had felt, held in, and was afraid to say, I said it. And I kept saying it.

Every morning and night I wrote everything I was holding in from years and years of suppressing. That, along with the positive belief that something would eventually change, and my consistent three-times-a-day guided meditations, helped me be out of pain in just three weeks. I couldn't believe it. After two years of having no answers, feeling hopeless, scared, and ready to give up on life, I was out of pain. How would I even be able to explain this to anyone?

" I decided to believe that somehow, somewhere, without me knowing the details, there would eventually be light if I kept looking."

You see, this was the part I was going to leave out of this book. My true dark night of the soul. The time when I was lying on my living room floor on my twenty-fifth birthday with my hands out to my sides, crying in extreme pain with no answers, looking up at the ceiling, wondering if I should even keep going. Wondering if this was it for me. The hesitation to leave this part out of the book came from a personal experience of going through something so dark, it felt impossible to believe there was light at the end of the tunnel. And when sharing a personal story, it's usually one's hope to create impact and change, but how can you convince someone else that there's light at the end of their dark tunnel? And the truth is, you don't need to. You don't need to be convinced. It's not about being convinced at first, it's about having belief. Because when I started the process of getting out of the darkest hole I had ever been in, I didn't get out of it by seeing any physical proof or evidence that there would be light. I actually had the complete opposite. I got out of it because I decided to believe that somehow, somewhere, without me knowing the details, there would eventually be light if I kept looking. And if there's one thing about me, it's that I'm a seeker. And on my journey of seeking, I realized I needed to become the person who was willing to show up and continue searching even when in pain, even when I felt like there were no answers. I knew, even though I couldn't see the light, I had to wake up every day as if there was light waiting for me. I had to wake up every day and become the version of me that knew this wasn't the end for me.

Starting anew every day

It's my belief that if I hadn't decided to get into a positive mindset by starting to have faith that something would change, and slowly start to change my habits while in pain, I would have never found that podcast and started a search for answers. If I didn't continue to go back to the doctors over and over, I would've had a harder time believing all the information I found on the mind-body connection.

If you are going through or have gone through a medical challenge also, although you may feel lost after exhausting every medical option, it is an important part of your healing journey. It is the commitment to seeking the answers and the continuation of getting back up and fighting for yourself that will create the space for answers to come.

After watching myself heal through the power of my mind, I knew I could no longer go back to the old me. After such a long journey with my hand pain and slowly regaining my independence, I knew this was the piece I needed to help me in the areas of my life that I was already struggling with before my chronic hand pain.

Every time I would fall off a diet, stop a workout routine, or completely just give up on a goal, I would go back to the old version of me that self-hated, self-sabotaged, and flat out never showed up for herself. With the wisdom I gained from having my life flipped upside down, I knew I couldn't do that again. I knew I couldn't fall back into setting unrealistic goals just so that I could fail. Going back to the gym just to change my body to get validation, going back on Instagram just to scroll and waste my life away, not reading books and educating myself now that I had my time back, not getting my finances in order, settling for less than I deserved, and full-on not going for exactly what I wanted in my life. I needed to finally glow up into the best version of me. And that is what I did. And that is what I hope for you. You see, after healing my chronic pain, I uncovered some of the deepest, most insightful healing practices and answers that were the missing links to my glow-up journey all along. I *needed* to go through this part of my life to deeply understand this incessant need to glow up, and how to once and for all heal and become the best version of me.

Reflection

Before getting into the second half of this book, I'd like you to think of something you're currently going through right now that you deem as "self-sabotage." I want you to get crystal clear on the thing you've been wanting to change so badly about yourself, or your life. I want this to be in the forefront of your mind as I take you through some of the most insightful processes to take when it comes to finally learning how to transform different areas of your life that you have always struggled with or deemed as "self-sabotage." Use the second half of this book as your guide to get out of your own way and transform your life whenever you feel stuck, unsatisfied, and like your glow-up journey is no longer moving forward.

PART II

PROJECT: YOU

CHAPTER FOUR

UNCOVERING ALL THE PARTS OF YOU

What's your motivation?

As humans we're meant to change and evolve, and there's no doubt that there's a part of every one of us that wants to go on some sort of journey of self-improvement, uplevelling and achieving our unique desires. But why do we tend to jump into journeys of self-development that feel like punishment? Why do we continue patterns of starting and stopping habits that are supposed to be good for us, such as eating healthy, working out, or doing meditation practices?

What I learned on my glow-up journey was that I was driven to change who I was from a place of self-hate and rejection. I was driven to clean up my diet and work out only as a means to an end goal which was, deep down, to meet an instinctual need to feel seen and to be loved. I started my journey with the idea that who I was was inherently wrong and bad, instead of starting a process of support and love for myself for everything I had struggled with and didn't receive in childhood. I often felt I was never enough and because I had this deep-rooted need to be chosen, I started to believe that to get that need met, I had to change.

Reflection moment

Think about a time where you felt unhappy with something in your life and you decided to do something to change that. Now think about the actual motive behind *why* you were so unhappy about it in the first place. Sometimes, it's simply because we know we haven't been taking care of ourselves or doing what's best for us without any real influence from those around us, but a lot of the times we're driven to change *only* to be liked by people who don't currently accept us for who we are, or *only* because someone decided to place their judgment on us based off their own preferences. I like to think of these two differences as internal motives and external motives. Both can have completely different outcomes based on our motivation behind it.

> **" The problem with changing from a place of self-rejection and the idea that you are inherently not good as you are right now is the habits and mindset that come with it. "**

The problem with changing from a place of self-rejection and the idea that you are inherently not good as you are right now is the habits and mindset that come with it. Instead of thinking about eating well, moving your body, or connecting with a network of friends out of a place of self-love and deservingness, we tend to tell ourselves we need to do these things as a form of punishment for who we are as human beings and that if we don't, we won't get what we want—which, deep down, is to belong.

Furthermore, I realized that the actions I was trying to take to change myself were coming from a part of me that I call "my inner critic"—someone who was a tyrant, a demander, a force not to be reckoned with. Something I also uncovered about my inner critic was that it mirrored the same type of harshness my father once had toward me. This inner critic of mine continued to get louder and louder in my head and would constantly tell me that I wasn't good enough. It told me I needed to change certain habits without caring at all how I felt during the process. My inner critic did not allow any room to question or ease up on the demands. That's where the restrictive fad dieting came along, the intense workouts, and the words of discouragement toward myself when I wasn't able to sustain such habits. Now if you think about it, what good comes out of trying to change something or someone through force and manipulation? How sustainable is it to try to change using pure punishment? When we hear it out loud, we realize how unloving and unsustainable that is, yet many of us continue to have this type of relationship with ourselves.

Truthfully, it's an unloving, selfish thing to not take into consideration that we have different parts of us that cannot uphold such harsh demands, along with parts of us that will not and should not be expected to be perfect or have it all figured out. The cherry on top that makes this stage of change even more difficult is that we also have a part of us that operates from a place of survival. You know, the part of me that went to candy to suppress her emotions? That part. The thing that stops our inner critic from succeeding in forcing ourselves to harsh standards is that this part—we can call it our inner child or our self-soother—will eventually dig its heels into the ground because it's convinced that the only way it can keep you safe from all of your unprocessed emotions (which never really go away because life in general can be stressful) is through the unfavorable behaviors it has picked up throughout your life. And until we start to address both our inner critic and inner self-soother, we will continue to reside within a mind and body that have immense amounts of disconnection and no true symbiotic relationship with one another.

Get real with yourself

It's my belief that the first stage of real change is to get curious and observe and learn how to address this relationship, or lack thereof, within ourselves. The inner critic part of us that self-hates and wants to change, but also the part of us that's more worried about survival and self-soothing and has been running on autopilot for years. What we fail to realize is that both of these parts actually want what's best for us, and in fact, they're not wrong for picking up and executing behaviors they believe will get you what you're longing for in life. But how they go about getting your needs met sometimes is not the healthiest. This includes the part of you that learned to eat candy or escape to protect you, or the critical part of you that embodies an unloving commander role that learned that the way to get accepted in society is through vanity metrics, and has been trying to achieve such vanity through unsustainable habits, negative self-talk, and an excessive need for external validation.

When I started to learn that I had two conflicting parts within me, I wanted to know how on earth I could get them to stop. How do we retrain these parts of ourselves to do things in a new way? How can we still reach our health goals while not feeling we are in prison the whole time? How can we stay consistent and have healthy habits as others do?

We want this process to feel less forced. We really want both parts to begin to heal and come together. We don't want to self-hate, we don't want to mindlessly self-soothe, and we don't want to wake up every day feeling like there is a constant internal battle happening within us that we have no control over. We want to finally glow up, be healthy, and become our own "it girl," but how?

Here's what I've found to be the most profound and helpful process to addressing this unhealthy relationship within us, which can keep us from having the ultimate, real, sustained glow-up.

1. Getting to know your inner world and understanding that your inner parts aren't here to sabotage your success and growth in life.

The most profound thing you can do on your journey of glowing up into the best version of yourself is to look at yourself as if you have different parts, personalities, childlike sides, etc., that are programmed and behave in ways that no longer serve you, but somewhere deep down are still convinced that they're keeping you safe. These parts are not actually against you; they've just picked up coping mechanisms that may no longer serve you and your truest desires. It's my belief that the most beneficial thing we can do on our glow-up journey is to first embody a sense of self-love and acceptance, instead of self-hate, toward the parts of us that have been acting out undesirable behaviors as our first step of truly glowing up into the person we desire to be.

2. Learning how to meet your needs and reparenting yourself.

After getting to know your inner world and embodying a sense of self-love and acceptance for all there is about you, your healing doesn't just stop there. There will still be things your inner parts need, and you will have to learn how to meet these needs in healthier ways. For instance, what you may find, like I did, is that deep down your inner critic just wants the best for you and has so many desires to grow and evolve, but never learned how to execute those desires in a healthy way. But as we learn to have a more loving, accepting energy toward ourselves, what usually ends up happening is that our inner critic no longer wants us to change from a place of punishment or hate. Instead, it wants us to change from a place of true self-love and growth, which means the actions it wants to implement to guide us along will no longer be as harsh and demanding as they once were.

3. Learning how to have a new relationship with yourself.

Acknowledging, forgiving, and accepting your inner parts for all the ways they've tried to protect you, while learning how to meet your needs in healthier ways, to me, is really what it means to have a healthy relationship with yourself. A healthy relationship consists of always taking the other person into consideration when doing certain actions because we know they can and usually will have some sort of effect on the other person. If we deeply love and support that person, we will want to do our absolute best to make sure our words and actions are from a place of love and support for them and us, and this is the same way we should be with ourselves.

Now you might be thinking, how do I actually form this new relationship with myself? How do I *do the work?* That is what we will explore next. I will take you through a few self-reflection practices to get closer to the root of your self-sabotage and guide you through ways to reparent yourself, while helping you uncover the shadows you have that are getting in the way of you becoming the person you've always wanted to be. And after that, we will talk about how to navigate some of the most impactful parts of our lives that play a huge role in our self-transformation journey such as friendships, family dynamics and environments, romantic relationships, limiting beliefs, and so much more, so that you can have the *ultimate* glow-up.

CHAPTER FIVE

REPARENTING YOURSELF

Understanding our
self-sabotage

" These behaviors are not intentional sabotage but more so efforts to self-soothe. "

Let's first look at self-sabotaging behaviors that get in the way of our goals. These are behaviors such as binging on processed foods, going back to a toxic ex, skipping the gym, procrastinating on our goals, etc. As we've uncovered, these behaviors are not intentional sabotage but more so efforts to self-soothe. Now, in order to change this unintentional self-sabotage, it's helpful to get to know your inner self-soother, why it's committed to such behavior, and what it needs instead. The truth is, we usually know our behaviors and the negative effects they have, but we don't necessarily know why there's a part of us that continues to do such behavior. Once we can see this part more clearly, this can give us a better opportunity to learn how to meet its needs in healthier ways.

Something I've found useful on my healing journey is to have inner conversations by simply asking the part of me that wants to behave undesirably. ***How does indulging in this behavior make you feel?*** At first it may seem like an odd concept, but the more times you start connecting to the parts of you that you've only ever learned how to be frustrated at, and instead learn to communicate in a more loving, compassionate space, you will start to receive some profound answers.

Now, this is only touching the surface of what Richard Schwartz calls Internal Family Systems Therapy. Essentially, it's a type of therapy model that believes we are made up of multiple "parts" or "personalities," which you can think of as having an internal family within yourself. This type of therapy suggests that the more you learn how to have "inner conversations" with parts of you that you have suppressed, the more true healing can occur. I would highly suggest looking more into the work of Richard Schwartz, starting with his book *No Bad Parts: Healing Trauma and Restoring Wholeness with the Internal Family Systems*. Being someone who has spent years using different psycho-therapy techniques, I truly believe the IFS model is the one that has helped me uncover parts of myself I didn't know existed the most. For the rest of the examples in this book, I will incorporate some of what I've learned over the years, including practices similar to Schwartz's "parts work," but my process is a very small piece of the bigger picture of IFS therapy. My hope is that the practices and insights I bring to you will be a good starting point for your healing journey.

What I found was that when I was a teen, lying in bed, scrolling Tumblr and eating candy made me feel safe, comfortable, and like I didn't need to be responsible for anything. I went further by exploring this part of me, thinking about where I might have first felt this feeling of wanting to escape, and I came to the realization that it was the same feeling I experienced when I was living with my father and there were so many rules and regulations I had no choice but to abide by. Although I didn't have the same rules placed on me by my father in my later years, the strict rules I put on myself to become this Tumblr girl and fit in always ended up becoming too much pressure in which I would crave escaping into the abyss of Tumblr, falling back into my comfort zone and pushing things off until Monday. This allowed me, for a moment, to feel some sort of release from the endless pressure, disempowerment, and unworthiness I felt on a daily basis.

After uncovering some truths as to why we are driven to self-soothe, the next question we can explore is, how do we stop these behaviors? Well, considering that what's driving these behaviors is our emotional states, it's important to learn how to meet our emotional needs in healthier ways.

A way I like to look at this is essentially a process of reparenting yourself. For me, I needed to figure out what it was going to take for this part of me to not feel so disempowered, lonely, and like it needed to escape all the stress and life challenges it still felt I was going through. The beauty of being in a state of reparenting is that we get to find new habits and behaviors that better suit some of our deep-rooted needs. During my healing journey, I realized I didn't get to experience the feeling of safety around a parent and environment that was best suited to my particular nervous system. I also didn't experience much freedom to make my own decisions, to go see my friends after school instead of being cooped up in my room. And simply, I had never experienced what it was like to feel worthy and enough as I was, instead of constantly being told (from my inner critic) that I wasn't enough and needed to constantly find ways to change myself.

" This is where your journey starts.
This is where the magic happens.**"**

So, with the understanding that we can't go back in time to change these core experiences and memories, how do we set ourselves free? How can we learn to deal with the stressors of life that we can't completely control in a healthier way? This is where your journey starts. This is where the magic happens. This is where, once you get to know your inner parts more, you can start to show up, stand up, and guide yourself through a process that no longer suggests to your inner soother that it needs to be in survival mode.

Here I have laid out a journal practice for you to explore ways to not only get to know your self-soother, but to meet its needs in much healthier ways. I encourage you, however, to use a blank journal for your healing journey in general to really dive deep and not be limited by the space in this book.

Journal practice

What behavior are you currently enacting that you don't want to be?

_____

_____

_____

_____

_____

_____

_____

_____

_____

_____

_____

_____

What usually prompts, triggers, or influences you to act out this undesirable behavior? (Think about the situation that occurs or the thoughts you think right before you have the urge to do these behaviors.)

How do these behaviors, although undesirable, benefit you? Or how do they make you feel in the moment you're doing them?

Here are some examples:

When I feel:

+ Lonely
+ Lost
+ Like a failure
+ Exhausted
+ Overwhelmed

Because:

+ I didn't get a text back
+ I didn't hit a goal
+ I didn't get enough sleep
+ Someone didn't show up in my life the way I wanted them to

I get the urge to:

+ Binge eat
+ Text my ex
+ Start all over on Monday
+ Skip the gym
+ Pick fights with loved ones

In the moment, these actions make me feel:

+ Happy
+ Less alone
+ Empowered
+ Safe
+ Comfortable

But soon after I act on my impulses, I eventually feel:

- ✦ Alone again
- ✦ Like all my health and fitness progress is lost
- ✦ Like my voice is not heard
- ✦ Behind in life

Example: When I text my ex, it's always after days of feeling alone, after dating men who don't make me feel the way I did with my ex, or when I feel no one is there for me. At that moment, sending that text feels good, but soon after when I get no response, or his response is not what I hoped for, I start to feel alone again. I start to feel unworthy again.

Now, change occurs when you start to become aware of the thoughts and feelings you experience right before you do such undesirable behavior, like in that example. And the healing starts to come when you learn how to soothe yourself in the moments before you take that undesirable action. Coming up with a list of things that you know make you feel happy and satisfied with your life is helpful on the days where you start to witness yourself wanting to go back to old behaviors.

Example: Things that make me feel less alone in my life are having girls' nights in, focusing on my goals and projects, journaling out my feelings when I'm upset, listening to uplifting music, making a list of the qualities I'm looking for in a future relationship, and taking care of my health and wellness.

Using the prompt and examples above, write out your own insights on the next page to the question posed on the previous page.

Your list of self-soothing techniques:

A question to help you figure out how to help yourself during times of unease is, "What activities or behaviors make me feel good about myself or help me in moments of emotional stress?" (See examples on page 88 if you need some ideas.)

_____

_____

_____

_____

_____

_____

_____

_____

_____

_____

_____

Here are some of the things you can do when feeling triggered, in hopes of sparking some ideas for your reparenting journey:

- **Having a positive self-talk journal session** by writing out what you're grateful for, telling yourself that you don't need to be perfect or rush your healing journey, or that even if you feel alone and unwanted right now, it doesn't mean that is the truth of how life will always be.

- **Watching people online who inspire you** to continue to love and better yourself.

- **Reading a book that gets you in a good mood.**

- **Meeting up with friend**s who you know love and support you.

- **Listening to music** that makes you feel good.

- **Cleaning** your space.

- **Signing up** for community events.

- **Getting yourself out** of your current environment.

- **Picking up a new hobby**, booking a therapy session, etc.

After making a list of things you know will make you feel better than how you would feel if you enacted on an unhealthy impulse, make a commitment to your inner self-soother that:

When I feel triggered and alone, instead of opening up my text conversation with my ex, I will first try texting my best friend to tell her about the impulse I'm feeling so she can remind me of why it may not be helpful to take that action, or simply to chat about something that has nothing to do with my ex to get myself off of this emotional rollercoaster.

Reminder: Your inner critic might come online and want to reparent for you. It might say something like "never get into a relationship again so that you don't get triggered, or just simply put down the candy and start a new restrictive diet when you feel an impulse to eat chocolate" will be the answer to getting you back into a better emotional state. Check in with yourself to see where this answer is coming from. Is it coming from your inner critic that wants to choose the most extreme option that you know is never really sustainable? Or is it coming from a part of you that sees how your self-soother really needs to experience feelings such as love, deservingness, and happiness, instead of feelings like isolation and constraint for having a natural, normal emotional response to something that's happened in your life, such as experiencing loneliness?

This is going to be a gradual process of change. You may not handle it perfectly every time. It will not always be as easy as saying "no" to an undesirable behavior. You have most likely been engaging in certain coping mechanisms for many years, so it's important that when you're learning how to reparent yourself that you simply witness yourself and your triggers before anything else. It's important that you be loving and kind with yourself when you're not able to make the "best" decision in the moment. This is when our inner critic tends to come online: when we set a goal to start reparenting ourselves and if we "fail" to meet our emotional needs in a "healthier" way. These are times when we tend to self-hate again. We want to move past this type of relationship with ourselves, as that is what keeps us stuck a lot of the time. If you're struggling heavily with learning how to meet your needs, reaching out for extra help from psychotherapists who specialize in IFS therapy or even somatic therapists in your area can be very beneficial on your journey to figure out what will really help you when you get triggered.

If you're struggling to have the financial means to access extra help from a psychotherapist, searching around online for psychotherapists who offer free resources and education to help you work through challenging moments in your life can be helpful. Here is a list of reputable mental health workers that offer free online resources, along with books or other affordable resources:

+ Dr. Nicole LePera, who goes by the name The Holistic Psychologist on social media. She offers many free healing workbooks, podcast episodes, affordable books, and YouTube videos

+ Nicole Sachs, LCSW, who provides free and paid resources all about healing emotional and physical pain; you can find her resources on any social media platform, and her podcast is called *The Cure for Chronic Pain*

✦ *The Mindful Movement* on YouTube provides thousands of free guided meditations to help ease anxiety and calm the mind, especially in moments when you're triggered

✦ Richard Schwartz, author of *No Bad Parts* and developer of IFS therapy

You can do this journal practice as many times as you need with the same issue, or you can use it to address another behavior, habit, or situation you'd like to help reparent yourself on. Something to also note is that you will naturally evolve and may even outgrow certain techniques after they've done what they've needed to do, so don't feel you have to be tied to any one technique or like you have to work to keep up with certain healing practices. The more you become self-aware and practice having this new loving relationship with yourself, you will start to trust and have a deep inner knowing of when it's time to shift from consistently relying on guided meditations or weekly therapy to get through every single trigger.

CHAPTER SIX

UNCOVERING YOUR SHADOW

Balancing self-improvement and self-acceptance

Now, reparenting in the form of meeting our emotional needs is only one side of the coin. The truth is, even as we learn to self-soothe, it doesn't mean other parts of us will be completely silenced, nor should they be. As I've mentioned, our inner critics are also crucial parts of us that are trying to keep us safe. When I say "safe," I simply mean our inner critics are actually here to help keep us on track of where we should go in life, and how we're going to get there. What usually happens is that somewhere on our journey through life, our inner critic has simply picked up the wrong beliefs about how to act, do, and be, which might not be the nicest, most helpful way to get us to our goals and desires in the long run. As we've seen, it can get very strict and harsh when it's time to evolve and change. One thing that I think many people get wrong on their self-love journey is thinking that they must love and accept every part of themselves to the point where nothing needs to change. But what I found as I started reparenting myself through meeting my emotional needs was that I still had a *desire for change*. I still needed some form of discipline and structure to help me not fall off my goals, even as I moved into a more self-loving, compassionate space.

So how can we have this balance? The balance between loving and accepting ourselves, while still pushing ourselves out of our comfort zones for evolution and change? Recognizing how important it is in a relationship to listen to where both sides are coming from and learning how to come to a conclusion that benefits both parties? The same way we took the time to understand our self-soother and what it needs, we also need to understand the programming behind our inner critics. For this process, we can essentially "retrain" and "reprogram" this part of us so that it's not so strict and domineering, but can still operate and guide us in a way that moves us forward in our evolution.

Let's look back at my own story. What I found was that my inner critic took on the consciousness of the strict and dominating energy of my father. I learned from a very young age that emotions were bad, not acceptable, and quite frankly useless. So every time I felt emotions coming up within me, I would instantly demonize them. **Become aware of your own inner critic and what voice or personality it embodies. What tone does it have? And when is it strongest?** My inner critic was also heavily influenced by what society deemed "acceptable" at the time; and because my inner critic wanted what was best for me, it unintentionally did harmful things, with the intention of protecting me. For instance, in my high school, pretty and thin girls seemed to get all the attention and popularity, and deep down, I wanted to feel wanted too. I correlated a certain body type with being accepted and loved. Because I didn't already look like that, the only way my inner critic thought we would achieve that feeling was to fully reject who I was and how I looked until I changed.

The thing you must understand about humans is that we have an innate drive to want to fit in and feel accepted, admired, and loved. But sometimes we're influenced by others around us. And unfortunately, the people who tend to influence us sometimes are people who also struggle with their own insecurities on how to achieve such desires. For instance, we might get taught that not only must we look picture-perfect to be accepted, but the way to achieve this must be perfect as well. Or we get taught that in order to change our bodies and become healthy, it has to be all or nothing. Essentially, we're all doing certain behaviors to achieve our goals, but it's important to take a deeper look to see the reasoning behind such goals, and if such behaviors are actually helping or hurting us in the process.

Let's take dieting and exercise as an example. On paper, working out six days a week with a rest day is known to be good for our health, and the science backs that up. Eating 80 to 100 percent unprocessed food is also something that will keep our bodies in optimal health which, again, is backed by science. Essentially, we get taught some sort of gold standard that we should be living up to, but why do we tend to fall short? Well, let's start with our inner self-soother. Our inner self-soother wants to keep us safe from uncomfortable emotions, which tends to lead us into falling into what feels like a pocket of comfort, but doesn't actually keep us safe because of how unhealthy it can end up being. We also have moving parts such as food accessibility, financial stressors, work-life balance, and things that can impair our ability to stick to a gold standard of living. For females, we have menstrual cycles where we operate on a twenty-eight-to-thirty-day calendar in which our hormones are fluctuating; this has a huge impact on the way our brains and bodies function. And overall, we come in contact and experience so many fluctuations in life, many of which we've never learned how to move through in a healthy way.

On the other hand, our inner critic has learned through social conditioning that the only way we are going to be worthy of love, attention, validation, or success is if we, let's say, fit into a certain body type or beauty standard. Not only do we start out ill-equipped for sticking to healthy habits due to our lack of ability to emotionally regulate, but the goals we set for ourselves tend to be extremely harsh and based on this incessant need to be accepted by society. So on one hand we must commend ourselves for wanting to go "all in" on a regime so that we can feel like we're part of society, loved, and wanted. But this type of mindset, when left unchecked, can lead us down a dark path of unnecessary perfectionism that convinces us we're keeping ourselves safe, but could be doing the complete opposite.

Reframing perfectionism

The perfectionist mindset, which you could say is the mindset our inner critic adopts, is something I've been fascinated by for many years as it's taken over so many areas of my life. The conclusion I came to was that the majority of the time it's hurting, not helping, us. Something I've realized is that the human desire to want to do things perfectly is actually less to do with doing a good job, and more about keeping ourselves safe from any perceived threat that would result from the lack of perfection (such as not being accepted by your chosen social group).

One helpful thing you can do on your journey is change the relationship you have with perfection. It's a little silly to expect ourselves to do things 100 percent, 100 percent of the time. For example, does it really make sense to expect a woman to perform at 100 percent in the gym while she's menstruating? No, but we call for it anyways. Or let's take our bodies for example. Throughout puberty and into adolescence, our bodies are constantly changing, yet we still expect ourselves to fit into size 00 jeans. Or even worse, when we're dealing with the loss of a loved one or a tough break up, we expect ourselves to "get over it" enough to show up to work and act like nothing happened.

> **"A hard, but freeing truth that I came to is that there are too many people on this earth for me to be everyone's cup of tea."**

Something that's really helped me move from this perfectionist mindset is realizing that perfection is simply an illusion; furthermore, looking at the long-term consequences of aiming to be flawless has actually led me further and further from who I'm trying to become. A hard, but freeing truth that I came to is that there are too many people on this earth for me to be everyone's cup of tea. I don't need to be. The desire to be picture-perfect emerged from the desire be loved and accepted by everyone, but the more I learned how to be there for myself and self-soothe during times of hardship, I came to find that I didn't actually need the entire world to fill the void I was experiencing. In fact, learning how to create a life filled with meaningful friendships, connections, and self-love was what I needed most. **Half of the people I was seeking love and validation from didn't even love themselves, let alone know how to love me, so why keep chasing something that wouldn't know what to do with my love when I presented it?**

"Nobody talks about how being a perfectionist creates this deep level of isolation."

The consequences of trying to be perfect were something that really started to hit me like a ton of bricks when I was struggling with my autoimmune disease. I realized every time I "fell" off my diet, I started spiraling and eating worse than if I had not been on any diet. The only time I had stomach issues was when I was hyper-focusing on how to stop having so many stomach issues. I also realized how much it was affecting my personal life. Nobody talks about how being a perfectionist creates this deep level of isolation. Being so hyper-fixated on every meal, every wellness routine, and reading every self-help book, left me no room to go out and have a social life. I couldn't even meet a friend for coffee if she was in town because I hadn't planned it a week before. I was too scared to go out for dinner with my friends because I couldn't control my meals, and when I did go out, I'd spend the whole time thinking about the food rather than connecting with my friends. It got to a point where I would rather stay in alone than go live my life. Now something that made the biggest impact with shifting out of the perfectionist mindset was learning how to self-accept, and realistically, be imperfect. But in order for us to do that, we need to learn where we picked up the harmful stories we tell ourselves about how we should look, act, and think.

Getting to know your shadow self

Let's talk about your shadow self, because she is the one that you've been running away from. Your shadow self is essentially all the parts of you that your inner critic learned to reject, hate, feel shame about, etc. The shadow self is based on what you've been taught and who you've been influenced by. So, let's say you've learned in school that it's undesirable to have belly fat or hip dips. If you haven't had a lot of self-worth instilled in you and helpful support at home, you might start hating on your body, dressing in ways that hide your "imperfections" so that you don't get made fun of and spend time figuring out ways you can change. But, if you didn't have such a predisposition to negative comments in the outside world because you were taught that you're very much valuable, even when someone thinks you don't fit into their beauty standard, you may not have such an adverse reaction to your natural body. Furthermore, you most likely wouldn't let someone dictate how you feel about your body by reminding yourself that just because your body isn't "desirable" to certain people, doesn't mean it's actually undesirable.

Having a strong, confident self-image is no easy task, especially as the media and many of our realities are constantly bombarding us with images and conversations around how we should look and feel. The most important thing to understand about unrealistic beauty standards and other people's negative opinions is that they don't come from a place of good intention. This includes the media wanting to capitalize on your insecurities or people trying to bring you down to make themselves feel better about their own insecurities.

There's a natural inclination to want to change and evolve, but there's a difference between changing something about yourself because you've thrown this part of you into your shadow, a.k.a. the "hate" pile, versus wanting to change out of love, out of a place of knowing certain practices and habits will enhance your quality of life. For instance, there's a huge difference between wanting to lose weight so that the boys in school like you better, versus wanting to lose weight because you've realized that it might be impacting the quality of your life and you really want to get yourself healthy again, *for you.*

Now depending on the influences you've had in your life, where you've grown up, the parents you had and more, you will have likely picked up many ideals and preferences on how you should look, act, and present in this world. It's not to say we shouldn't be influenced to show up in life a certain way, but when things move into the realm of self, rejecting something that is natural to us or that we want to change simply to gain acceptance rather than for our quality of life, or how it makes us feel regardless of the validation we will or will not get, that's when we should take a look at where we first picked up these ideals and explore whether we want to continue to hold these as truths for ourselves. **That's what you'll do next.**

Journal practice

What do I judge, criticize, and/or not accept about myself and others?

_____

_____

_____

_____

_____

_____

_____

_____

_____

_____

_____

_____

What are my first memories of when I picked up these judgments and thoughts about myself and others?

Example: I judge myself for having hip dips, along with judging others who resemble the same body type as me. I created a story in my head that only girls without hip dips are desirable because in school, only the girls without hip dips get chosen, praised, and loved. I also see on social media all the girls with perfect body types getting praise and attention that I wish I could have.

Is this the full truth and do I have to continue to keep this part of me (the fact that I have hip dips) in my shadow and continue to self-reject?

Example: I do know some girls who don't have the body type that is praised and do receive attention and love. Lately, I've been seeing my body type represented on social media. So I guess this isn't the full truth of what it means to be desirable, but it's just something that I've been taught.

_____

_____

_____

_____

_____

_____

_____

_____

_____

_____

_____

_____

_____

_____

_____

_____

_____

_____

How can I own and start to accept parts of my shadow self?

Example: I can start speaking to myself positively and reminding myself I don't have to look like other girls to be likable and accepted. I can remind myself that I'm not the only one with this certain body type and that so many other girls have it too, and many of them feel super confident within their own skin. I can stop hanging around people who only care about looks. I can focus on the things that make me feel good about myself like doing my schoolwork, projects, focusing on my goals, taking care of my body through eating well and moving, and connecting with friends who love and support me.

Make a commitment to yourself: Every day I will do one thing to help me start to reintegrate my shadow self, which will be:

Example: Every day, I will journal three affirmations that make me feel more accepting and loving about my body. I will also take some time this week to unfollow people who don't support my body image and how I'd like to look at myself. I will continue to check in with myself when I feel the desire to work out and eat well and guide myself back to remembering the positive aspects of taking care of my health and wellness outside of what it will do for me externally, which will be fleeting after a few months of surface-level attention that I might get if my body does "fit in" to a certain beauty standard. I will remind myself of all the benefits of taking care of my health, such as having more energy in the morning to complete tasks at school or work, how great my mental health is when I'm active and fueling my body with healthy foods, or even how comfortable I feel in my body when I'm strong and able to spend hours on a hike or bike-riding with my friends during the summer months.

CHAPTER SEVEN

REBUILDING SELF-CONFIDENCE

Cleanse your social media

When I started exploring the roots of my insecurities, I realized that one of the biggest players was social media. **Remember when I said, "it all started with Tumblr"?** I wasn't kidding. I realized the amount of time I spent online looking at bodies that weren't mine and faces that didn't resemble me heavily contributed to the breakdown of the little confidence I did have. Although I think living a life off social media isn't mandatory to heal your relationship with your self-image, it could definitely help. But if you're someone like me who realistically can't and doesn't want to live off the grid, I invite you to start taking inventory of all the accounts you follow and people you watch, and analyze the imaginative self-concept you've been creating and that you may be trying to live up to.

> " We all need to see women who look, dress, and act like us receive love on social media and access to opportunities just like the rest. "

Throughout my healing journey, I started to realize I wasn't following or looking up to anyone with the same body type, hair texture, or skin color as me. This is not to say that you can't be inspired and motivated by others who don't look like you, but it's been beneficial to see that there is beauty in my own features. We all need to see women who look, dress, and act like us receive love on social media and access to opportunities just like the rest. The more often we see ourselves as successful and happy people, the less we feel the pressure to have to change and conform. And when learning how to rebuild your self-worth and image, it's important that you're surrounded by positive messaging and representation of who you are, or who you can become.

> **" I was able to appreciate and see the beauty and uniqueness in others while simultaneously choosing and loving myself."**

The more intentional I got with the images and content I was consuming on social media, the more self-acceptance and peace I felt within myself. On top of that, as the years went by and I built up my self-confidence, when I did get exposed to images that used to trigger me, they no longer made me feel bad about myself. I was able to appreciate and see the beauty and uniqueness in others while simultaneously choosing and loving myself. I learned to no longer look up to people from this place of inferiority; I no longer needed to experiment with different makeup looks, hairstyles, or outfits from a place of pure self-rejection. I'm now able to love myself for who I am, while continuing to explore my natural desire to want to grow. I know that when I'm looking my best and all dolled up, I'm just as beautiful and worthy of acceptance and love as when I'm not the most picture-perfect, glowed-up version of myself.

Now this change didn't happen overnight; it might not for you either, and that's okay. But one thing to understand is that rebuilding your self-confidence is going to essentially be up to you. Is it unfair and unhealthy that social media's impact on us can be negative at times? Yes. Is it unfair that we might have grown up or are surrounded by people who judge, criticize, and project their own insecurities onto us? Absolutely. But my hope is to empower you with mindset shifts and guidance on how you can re-empower yourself so that you're better able to navigate in this world without losing yourself.

If you're on a journey of rebuilding your self-image and confidence and you find social media, or your social circles, have had a big impact on you, here are some of my best tips to protect your peace and learn to change the way you see yourself.

Protecting your peace

✧ **Consider unfollowing or muting accounts that trigger you** to the point where all you want to do is change yourself. When you're no longer motivated to take action and instead find yourself gazing and obsessing over someone else's looks or life, that's a good indicator to take a pause. There came a point on my journey where I got entirely sick of sitting around, gazing over people who looked and had what I wanted and instead started to take self-loving action toward the girl I knew I wanted to be, which was the best version of me, not the best version of someone else. It's time you do the same.

✧ **When spending time on social media, look for people who resemble you, post positive and uplifting content, indulge in healthy behaviors such as balanced eating and workouts, and speak on topics that help you**

become a better person, instead of following people who simply only show how perfect their life is, or maybe flaunt their bodies or achievements without really giving you any helpful tips to help you on your journey. Again, there is absolutely room for inspiration and motivation, but making sure you balance that by taking that motivation and fueling it for action within your own life is crucial. Putting time limits on how much content you're going to consume, along with diversifying the type of content you consume, can be helpful as well. When on social media, I spend the majority of my time watching videos or consuming content that teaches me something, versus only showing me how amazing someone else's life is. It's important to witness how much "motivational" content you consume without taking any real action.

✧ **Have a morning practice that is all about you.** Do this by writing out, or verbally speaking, all the things you've accomplished, all the amazing qualities you hold, and all the things you like/love about yourself on not only a physical level, but mental. Becoming your own best friend each and every morning by hyping yourself up and reminding yourself of your own worth is going to be a job that only you can do, and that you should do. This at first might be hard, especially when you feel like there's not much about you to praise, but understand this: reprogramming negative thoughts that run on autopilot will take some consistent conscious effort from you to change them.

Writing a list of amazing qualities that you hold one day a week when you've been subconsciously reading off a list of "reasons to hate myself" every day for over ten years isn't going to change how you think about yourself throughout the rest of the day after you've finished this practice. That's why it's so helpful to create repetition by doing this first thing in the morning, anytime you start to feel those negative thoughts creep up, or even at night to give yourself that reminder. Something I like to do when a negative, critical thought pops into my head is to say, "this is simply an old negative belief that I picked up when I was young, based off of false pretenses that no longer serve me and no longer need to be my truth," while persisting in a new belief about myself that I want to hold. It's important that you continue to redirect your mind when you find it wanting to go back to an old thought and recognize that this is simply your inner critic trying to keep you safe by doing what it thinks is best to keep you safe. Thank your inner critic for trying to keep you safe, while lovingly persisting in a new story.

✧ **Remind yourself that just because someone else is beautiful, successful, or wanted by others, that doesn't make you any less valuable than them.** In fact, someone else's beauty, success, and life shouldn't have anything to do with you. At times it can feel like we aren't as worthy as someone who we might not be on the same level as, but instead of comparing or competing, use them as a source of inspiration and motivation that you can become (in similar ways) just like them. Check in with yourself when you do start to use such people as inspiration though, as we never want to try and be a carbon copy of someone else. Understanding that we will always be influenced by others, but that we are unique and people will love and accept us for such uniqueness, is the most important thing we should be reminding ourselves of. Something I like to tell myself when I find I've been a little too motivated or inspired by someone to the point where I'm starting to look at myself as "less than" is to remind myself that originality and uniqueness will always win. Trying to be the person you're looking up to, to a T, won't work because there's something about them that you can't possibly copy, but the reverse is also true. You have something so special that can't be taken away from you. So home in on what that is, nurture that uniqueness, explore it, and embrace it.

✧ **This leads me to my last point: start embodying and expressing the real version of you.** Which yes, will be flawed, and guess what? That's okay. This might look like letting yourself cry in your room if you've been someone who's always demonized your emotions because quite frankly, you're kidding yourself if you think that you'll live a life emotion-free. This also might look like walking around your room with a bikini on, learning how to feel comfortable in your own skin instead of hiding and covering yourself, even if you're not super happy with what you see in the mirror. Instead of picking out your flaws in that mirror, practice pointing out one thing that you like or love about yourself instead of instantly going to the negative. Or even start showing yourself what's possible when you go out into the world; instead of doing your hair and makeup to the nines, try a laid-back look, which realistically saves you time and effort and might be something you've been dying to do. See the reactions you get, or quite frankly don't get, when you step outside. What you'll find is that no one cares. No, seriously; no one cares if you're done up or not. This is not to say it doesn't matter or that you shouldn't make yourself feel good by getting ready every day or wearing something that makes you feel amazing; it's simply to show yourself it's possible to exist in both worlds. There's nothing more empowering than being confident within yourself to go out in public all dolled up, or wearing no makeup at all, and still know you're as worthy and lovable. The more you experiment with letting yourself be and look many different ways around many different people, I really do believe it allows you to feel the most confident you can be. My wish is for you to continue pushing yourself in new ways by showing yourself it's possible to not only be loved and valued for being you, but simply that you are *safe*, being you.

Friendships inventory

Although social media can have such a huge impact on us and how it forms our self-image, so can our social circles. The people we surround ourselves with offline can heavily impact the way we think about ourselves and others. When I started to look at my social life, I noticed that a lot of the girls I grew up with were no longer on the same path as I was. I realized that we weren't really interested in the same topics such as bettering our lives, taking responsibility and accountability for our actions, learning how to love ourselves and others better, etc. As much as I tried to stay in a tight-knit circle by continuing to go out and party every weekend, negatively gossip and complain about how crappy life was, and indulge in hookup culture like we had been, I knew that I needed to stop.

> **" I knew that if I wanted to continue on a journey of deep self-love, and not be fueled to change from a place of insecurities and competition with others, I had to rethink the friendships I had and the boundaries I didn't have."**

I knew that no matter how much I tried to hold myself to a high standard, when I was around certain friends and put myself in these social situations, it was incredibly hard for me to stand my ground and have boundaries. It was incredibly hard to not self-criticize and judge myself when my entire friend group was not only doing the same, but our sole bonding experiences were around our looks, who could date the hottest guy, and how popular we were on social media. I knew that if I wanted to continue on a journey of deep self-love, and not be fueled to change from a place of insecurities and competition with others, I had to rethink the friendships I had and the boundaries I didn't have.

The truth is, many of us can't escape social media, or people in real life. We are surrounded by so many human beings with different thoughts, beliefs, and insecurities. On one hand, we should always be trying our best to seek out friends and social groups that make us feel better, not worse about ourselves, but what I've found helpful throughout my glow-up journey and navigating social circles is to learn to have boundaries. If you don't learn to develop boundaries within relationships, even the healthy ones, you may start to find yourself pleasing people or worse, morphing yourself into whatever the group's identity is. As I've mentioned, it's not a bad thing to be influenced by friends or social media or to want to be a part of the clique, but when you start to lose your identity by slowly rejecting all the natural and unique parts of your physical appearance and personality, it's time to rethink who you let into your life and infiltrate your mind.

The start of my assertion of my boundaries came in the form of simply no longer being available for party weekends and complaining sessions. No longer saying yes to plans or conversations that I knew did not serve me mentally or physically. But one thing I wish someone would've given me advice on when it came to boundaries and my social life was how to set them when I'd already created years' worth of friendships with people. Also, where would I find friendships that did serve me?

"A lot of the time, not setting boundaries and people-pleasing is simply another self-soothing technique that our inner self-soother has picked up from when we were young."

When it comes to setting boundaries, this can be challenging for many of us for many reasons. A lot of the time, not setting boundaries and people-pleasing is simply another self-soothing technique that our inner self-soother has picked up from when we were young. Many of us who struggle with having a voice, saying no, or communicating our needs simply have never had the experience of being able to do so in a healthy way. For me, I learned from a very young age not to speak up and say how I'm feeling because if I did, my father would punish me. In our household, my voice really didn't matter. So naturally, I learned that my voice never mattered and that if I did speak up for what I believed or expressed my feelings, there were consequences. Remember, the part of us that learned to pick this behavior up still doesn't know it's in different situations now, where it might be way more safe to express its needs. Even if this part of you does know that it's able to express its feelings now that you're an adult, it's never even had practice doing so.

So here are my best tips on learning how to set boundaries when it comes to social groups and friendships that, deep down, you know are affecting your self-image and the direction you're trying to take in life. I've also included my best advice when it comes to figuring out how to find new friendships that serve you.

Making friends and creating boundaries

◇ **When coming to the realization that your friendships are not serving you, it's important to consider the vision you hold for yourself, your life, and especially your relationships.** Getting clear on where you see yourself in the next three to five years, where you want to be spending your free time, and the type of people you want to be surrounded by is a crucial part of building, maintaining, adjusting, or even letting go of friendships. If you don't know what it is that you're looking for in a friendship, it's going to be hard for you to express or communicate such needs when the time comes. For me, I started to get honest with myself and realized that I felt so much better on the days where I wasn't hungover from a night out of partying, or spending my entire evening before an event hyper-focusing on how to look the hottest when going out or chatting about which boys were on- or off-limits. I realized that I loved waking up early in the morning, hangover free, meeting up with my friends to go for a beautiful morning walk, chatting about positive aspects of our relationships, or gushing over our favorite influencers that inspired us. I loved spending time during the day going to a workout class or planning an early-evening dinner that didn't involve heavy drinking. I loved planning weekend cottage trips and vacations where the main event was laying out by the beach and reading *The Summer I Turned*

Pretty instead of getting the perfect bikini shot. Now for you, where you want to spend your time with your friends might be different than my desires, and that's okay. My point here is to prompt you to think about the type of friendships, the quality of conversations you want to have, and where you want to spend your time, which is key for the next step.

✧ **After getting clear on the types of friendships you're wanting to call into your life, it's going to be important for you to take inventory of your current friendships.** Now, this is not to say your friends need to be perfectly aligned to the vision you hold for yourself, nor should they be, but evaluating whether some of your friends seem to be on the same path as you is going to be crucial for when it's time to communicate. The truth is, some of our friends aren't on the same path as us, and quite frankly it's not their time to change that path. Something I had to realize is that it wasn't my job to force my friends to see the world as I do. It's not my job to convince them why they should be spending their mornings walking by the water, talking about our goals versus spending time at bars and texting their exes. Although there's always room to support our friends as they move through their phases of life, if their phase of life isn't aligned to ours, this is when it's important to have conversations with such friends.

When I was younger and decided to get super clear on the vision I held for my life, I realized there were many people who most likely wouldn't be coming on that path with me.

When coming to that conclusion, I thought it would be better to stop putting in effort into these friendships by simply cancelling plans last minute, not answering phone calls, and pretending everything was fine even when it wasn't, simply because I didn't care to continue to maintain that friendship. And although that might seem like the easy way out in the moment, not only are you hurting someone that you once formed a friendship with, you're actually creating an unhealthy pattern within your style of communication and friendship-building that will follow you into the next friendship when you feel that friendship needs work. That's what happened to me. I started looking at a lot of my friendships that weren't up to my standards as easily disposable. And although this is not to say that you have to work on a friendship you know deep down is no longer for you, I think when we're talking about truly glowing up into the best versions of ourselves, the best versions of ourselves would be ones that aren't afraid to communicate, ones that give others respect, ones that take accountability.

✧ **Take accountability, communicate, and make it about you.** When deciding to either work on a friendship through healthy boundaries or simply end one, it's so important when communicating to your friends that you express your desires, needs, and wants, versus blaming them for all of their downfalls and how they make you feel. The reason this is so important is that it always takes two. It took you entering a friendship with low boundaries, or old interests that no longer serve you, along with the other person's part. This is not to blame yourself for the breakdown of the friendship and how it turned out, but blaming another person entirely for your unhappiness, in my opinion, is not something the best version of yourself would do.

✧ **For the friends you want to keep, communicating about your future, your goals, how you want to spend your time and why, and where you'd love to spend your time instead, is a good start to potentially creating change within a friendship.** The thing is, when realizing you want things to change in your life, you can't expect your friends to read your mind or change the minute that you do. Give it time and see what your friends think. I found on my journey that the more I expressed how I wanted to spend my time doing healthier activities and engage in healthier conversations, a lot of them wanted the same.

✧ **To the friends you want to let go of, it's important to make your decision before entering a conversation with a friend with whom you have a codependent type of dynamic.** If you leave the door halfway open by expressing the above tip, without also letting them know that you no longer feel that this friendship is serving you and you're wanting to move on, you might end up in a friendship where this person says that they want exactly what you want, but just ends up going back to their old ways and you're stuck in the same pattern. It's important to recognize such patterns and express that you're not interested in repeating that pattern.

✧ **Stop saying things you don't mean.** This last tip is one of the most helpful for setting boundaries. Stop saying you like spending your Friday nights at a bar when you don't. Stop judging other women and jumping on the hate train with your friends when deep down, you actually don't hate that girl like the rest of your friends. You've once learned to be quiet and nice and not express your true feelings, but that's over now. When you start to witness your inner self-soother wanting to say yes to things you don't want to do, try to engage in an inner dialogue, saying something such as, "I see you; you want to agree because you're afraid if you don't, they won't like you. I know you're just trying to keep us safe, but if we continue to say yes, we will end up being in a friendship that makes us more unsafe. It's okay to express my true feelings, and if they don't like it, they were never for us anyways."

Finding better friends

On our journey of creating better friendships, we will find that sometimes yes, our friendships end, or they fade away the more we start putting our time and attention into things that serve us more. In these times, it's really important that we remind ourselves we can and will find better friends. *But where?* Many of the reasons why it took me so long to let go of unhealthy friendships were because I had no one else to do things with, so I would have rather done things that I barely liked instead of spending my time alone.

Here's my best advice when it comes to finding new friends that align with your goals.

✧ **Many times, you meet people where you're at in your life.** Meaning, when you're spending your time and energy in environments that do not serve you, it's no wonder you meet people who are only aligned with those environments, like drinking at bars. This doesn't mean that people can't go out and have a good time and end up being lifelong friends, especially when it's once in a blue moon that they go out to places that aren't their normal cup of tea. But the more time you spend in places where you'd ideally want to be with friends, chances are that you will run into people who are much more aligned. Take inventory of where you spend most of your time. It will likely be at work, school, or at the same two coffee shops a week. If you want to experience new people in your life, it's time to make a shift. Start going outside for lunch instead of eating your lunch at the normal cafe spot at your work or school. Start saying hi to the few people who you almost always walk past during work or school, but don't. Start planning one day out of the week to work at a new coffee shop or eat at a new cafe that's outside of your normal routine. Simply moving yourself out of the same four walls will allow room for potential new friendships to open up.

✧ **Another thing I had to get real with myself about when it came to making friendships was how open I actually was to making friends.** As much as we all say we want new, more meaningful connections with others, we are sometimes deathly afraid of letting people in. Exploring the self-sabotaging behaviors you tend to have when it comes to building friendships can be helpful if you find yourself backing out at the last minute, or if you've made a new friend at work and exchanged numbers, but continue to put off confirming your out-of-office coffee date.

✧ **Is your energy open? Are you curious?** When it comes to recognizing how open you are to new friendships, energy is something people can feel. When you're walking down the street, are you genuinely open with your energy? Meaning, are you making eye contact with people? Are you smiling? Are you petting that dog that's always coming up to you in which the owner could easily be your new best friend if you just stopped for a second and let that love in? What about that girl you see every day at your gym who seems the same age as you, who always wears the cutest workout sets, but you insist on keeping such a compliment to yourself? You'll be surprised at just how much *curiosity* can be a door opener for long-lasting friendships. Many of us make meeting new people more complicated than it needs to be when really, opening our energy on our walks home from the office, in the gym, or simply putting ourselves in new environments is all the universe needs us to do to be aligned to the people who really serve us.

✧ **Making and maintaining friendships isn't always a walk in the park.** We have a list of wants, needs, and expectations from the types of friendships we make. On one hand, it's very healthy to have expectations, but something that's helped me not get too overly attached, emotional, or disappointed when my friends don't act, think, or be according to my imaginary list of expectations is to learn to detach from outcomes. The more pressure you put on yourself or another person to show up a certain way in a friendship when life inevitably happens and when either of you can't show up the way you've pictured your friendship to look on paper, the more likely this will create arguments, grudges, or negative opinions on the future of our friendships because we've been so attached to the outcome of what this friendship needs to look like. The reality is, friendships take time, they're messy, they're confusing, and no one gets it perfect. Detach from the perceived outcome of what you think someone should do or be for you all the time, and allow your friendships to be what they're meant to be at times, *imperfect*.

Learning to express my needs in friendships, no longer saying yes to things I don't want to do, and aligning myself by putting myself in new places and opening up my energy has allowed the universe to bring me the most amazing, beautiful, dynamic friendships in my life that look nothing like what I thought they would be, you know... the ones in the movies? What I've found is that my friendships are better than the ones in the movies because they're real. And not only that, the type of friendships I've built have indirectly influenced the steps I take in my life and how I look at myself. **I find myself spending time in environments that serve me, having**

conversations that motivate me, and consistently receiving beautiful words of affirmation from my friends that help build up my self-worth, rather than tear it down. It's my hope that you take a good look at the people you surround yourself with when it comes to glowing up into the best version of yourself, implement some of my best tips, and watch your life transform.

Romantic relationships

A lot of the advice I've given you can easily be applied to romantic relationships, but of course they're usually much more dynamic. You see, we tend to get into relationships with people based on what we believe we deserve from a partner. On top of that, it's my belief that we tend to crave the love of the person we were craving love from in childhood, or subconsciously recreating relational dynamics from past caregivers. Although these dynamics that we experienced in childhood were not in the form of romantic relationships, our closest relationships with our caregivers still set the tone for how we learn to have any sort of relationship in our adult lives. For example, I was used to being around a father who was very distant, dominant, powerful, and made all the decisions. And while I didn't feel safe and didn't enjoy being around that type of man, I was very used to being around that type of behavior and he subconsciously taught me that this is just how men are. So when I went out in my adult life and started to date, the men that I felt a sense of normalcy around had those same qualities because that was what I was used to, and what I was taught men should be like.

Another thing I experienced in childhood was not receiving a lot of validation, acceptance, and love from my father, which in turn always had me wondering what was wrong with me and why I wasn't getting accepted by him. What I did learn was that if I listened to the rules, did what he said, and acted like a good girl, I would be in his good books. Subconsciously, I did that with men too. I never thought that being just me was enough, so naturally I always tried to fit this mold (which was taught to me by society) of what the ideal woman would be for a man to want to love; I tried doing it but failed every time. My core wound was that in order for me to get love, I needed to conform and be someone I was not.

Now, if I was taught by my father that I didn't need to change for anyone, and that getting love from him and him showing up in my life was a normal, consistent thing, I would have more easily resonated with, recognized, and been attracted to that type of treatment from men in my adult life. Furthermore, the ones who didn't accept me, didn't show up, or didn't want to treat me well would have been pushed to the side as I would've known that those are not the men for me. Instead, I learned those were the men I should try and seek love from, since that was the mission I'd been on since I was a little girl.

It took me a long time to realize that not only did I not have a healthy father figure in my life, which would impact my romantic relationships, but once I got into relationships with these types of men who were expressing a lack of love the same way my father did, I came to realize time and time again that there was actually no love to be given no matter what mold I tried to fit into for them, because these men didn't even love themselves. I realized that I was trying to prove how lovable I was to someone who obviously had no idea how to express love or receive it in the first place and no matter how close I got, I wasn't going to change that. I also realized that it wasn't my job to convince a man to see my worth, or to teach him how to love me. I realized that the more I said no to relationships that didn't feel good to me by mere fact of always feeling put to the side, disappointed, or not shown up for, the better I felt. I felt better not trying to convince or chase someone who didn't have the capacity to love me. And what I really realized was that it was never, ever personal. The reason someone isn't able to love me, or see beauty in me, or show up for me, is because of their own internal state of being, their own narratives, their own upbringing, their own trauma. Something I also came to understand was that I wasn't the only one who struggled with loving themselves or came from a traumatic past; it's everyone else, too. So why take it personally? Why spend years trying to fix and heal someone who is not willing to do the work themselves in hopes that one day they will love you? *Respectfully,* respect yourself and stand in your worth, my love.

With that said, there are going to be people in your life, especially in romantic relationships, who of course have these backgrounds but may be absolutely healthy enough to stay with and support on their journey. That will require them to see themselves fully, and commit to doing the work. And of course, there are going to be people that you realize just aren't healthy enough for you to continue staying with. After working through some of the subconscious beliefs I held about myself—for example, how I wasn't lovable or wasn't worthy of being shown up for, which came up during the times of a hard breakup—I started to come up with a few key questions to ask myself when dating. The motive for these questions was to make sure that I was not letting my inner self-soother drag us back into relationships that no longer served us and allow me to discern whether I should stay committed in such a relationship or let it go.

Journal practice

Here are the questions you can ask yourself and reflect on too:

How do I *feel* when I'm with them?

_____

_____

_____

_____

_____

_____

_____

_____

_____

_____

_____

_____

Do they show up in my life consistently?

Am I recreating old patterns or attachment styles from past relationships or family dynamics?

Is this person on the same page as me mentally?

_____

_____

_____

_____

_____

_____

_____

_____

_____

_____

_____

_____

_____

_____

_____

_____

_____

_____

_____

_____

_____

_____

_____

_____

_____

_____

_____

_____

_____

_____

_____

Outside of what they do for me conditionally (such as taking me on dates, buying me gifts, or sending text messages with a bunch of promises for the future), how do I feel about this person when they're not giving me these things?

Do I enjoy their company even if we aren't on a fancy date? Do they take action on the words they send me through text?

These questions can help you gauge whether you're gaslighting yourself into staying in a relationship that is more of an unhealthy pattern you need to break free from by stepping into your own self-worth, or potentially understanding that this is a real relationship that could flourish into something beautiful the more you continue to step into your worth with a person who has committed to you and is willing and wanting to do the work with you.

One last thing I'll say about romantic relationships: We sometimes tend to put all the blame and focus on the other person and what they're not doing or how they're not treating us, and although it can be very useful to identify how you're feeling and address these concerns, it's always important to see how you're playing a role in this undesirable dynamic, because it always takes two. Taking accountability in your relationships can help shift your undesirable circumstances in a few ways: One, it might help and influence your relationship in a positive direction, or two, you start to step more into your self-worth, work on the things you've been letting slide, and naturally you will create more space for people to come into your life who can give you what you deserve, as the ones who don't will naturally fade away because you're no longer holding space for them.

Journal practice

Here are a few questions to ponder when it comes to taking accountability in your own romantic relationships:

How much time have I been focusing on the negative things they're doing, versus all the things that I'm doing?

What role am I playing that contributes to this undesirable outcome?

How can I actively work on the role that I'm playing (which doesn't involve trying to change this person)?

What are things that I've been slacking on, or losing focus on, that I could be putting my time and energy into outside of hyper-fixating on my partner and their imperfections?

How can this relational dynamic reflect what I believe and feel about myself?

Just like friendships, romantic relationships are no walk in the park. They require a level of self-awareness from both parties in order to really make it work, or to potentially move in different directions. Whatever the direction may be, the best version of you is intentional, self-aware, accountable, and communicates. The more you step into this version of you, the type of people you start to attract, or the dynamic within your current relationships, will not only change, but they will greatly impact your own self-image and the direction you continue to take in your life. Just watch.

Family dynamics

"And the truth is, we don't have control over these people or situations, but we have control over ourselves and where our focus goes."

During my college years, my home life became my biggest trigger and challenge. I was faced with the reality of living with a mother who was struggling heavily with addictions, and I was surrounded by an environment that wasn't healthy, stable, or secure. Maybe your environment isn't as unsafe as mine was, but many of us live in environments that we sometimes aren't able to leave and get out of, and it can make us feel like we have absolutely no control over these situations or people. And the truth is, we don't have control over these people or situations, but we have control over ourselves and where our focus goes. One thing I learned early on in my journey was as much as I wanted those around me to change so that I could feel safe and so that they could get better, it was not my responsibility to change them. Continuing to try to do so was burning me out and creating more stress and anxiety than the circumstances at hand. Another thing I learned was that sometimes the environment or situation is too big to try to fix, and instead of trying to fix something outside of me, bringing my attention and focus onto myself became the most empowering thing I could have ever done.

After years of living in an unhealthy, unstable environment, I started exploring what would happen if instead of waking up every day, hyper-focusing on everyone's actions and wrongdoings, I started witnessing the stories I kept telling myself about my life and started telling myself a more positive, helpful story while keeping my focus and attention on what I could change in those moments. I recognized that the less I would focus on my negative circumstances, the better I felt. I decided to stop focusing on how crappy my homelife was, how disadvantaged I was because my mother at the time was an addict and my father had passed away during high school, the fact that I had no one holding my hand and helping me through life, and how everything wasn't perfect in my life the way I thought it was for everyone else. Most importantly, I stopped spending my time being angry at people and circumstances that weren't in my favor, and instead I started to *reframe.*

> **"I really started transforming myself into a person who lived the life I always dreamed of, *before I even had it.*"**

I started looking at my life story as a lesson, as a phase of my life, as a story that I was going to tell one day, and guess what? *This day is now.* I started focusing on all the big and small things that kept me sane, like my ability to think clearly so that I could make a gratitude list every morning and read books that would allow me to learn more about life. I started to create goals and action plans on how I was going to build my credit, buy a car, get out of debt, and go to school so I could live the life I'd always dreamed but didn't get handed. I started learning how to cook for myself, keep my environment clean, and work out so that I could feel good on a day-to-day basis. I really started transforming myself into a person who lived the life I always dreamed of, before I even had it. This at times was no easy task. I had many days where I broke, I had many days where my nervous system was so dysregulated that I wasn't able to think clearly and show up for myself. I had many days where I also struggled with asserting my boundaries, making the "right" and most self-loving decision for me. On those days I decided I no longer wanted to do what I used to do, which was self-hate, negatively talk down to myself for not being perfect, and fall back into this inner critic that I knew was simply just the old version of me trying to stay safe. On those days, I allowed myself to cry, to mourn the loss of the relationship I wasn't experiencing with my mom and would never get from my father, to let myself feel angry at the world for having such crappy situations play out in my life. If there's a life circumstance so big that you can no longer control, you can let it out too. This is the thing—you don't need to be strong every second of every day; quite frankly, it's impossible. What matters is the loving energy you put back toward yourself on the days where life feels a little too hard, and most importantly, how you pick yourself back up when you're down.

Here's how I navigated living in toxic environments and around people who weren't on the same journey as me, in hopes of helping you if you're in a situation that's undesirable.

Family housekeeping

✦ **One of the first things I had to do when I was faced with the reality that I was living in an environment with a mother who was deeply struggling, and recognizing that the environment I was living in really started to affect my mental and physical health, was to reach out for help.** I connected with family members and close friends to get support, I had open and honest conversations with my mother, and I started going to therapy to help me manage the stressful environment I was living in. Now this is going to depend on the situation you're in, but I want to make it incredibly clear that although there are so many things we may have control over when helping us navigate hard phases of our lives, reaching out for support and not going through such circumstances alone is crucial. You are not meant to handle hard things in your life alone, even if it feels like no one is around. There were many times where I had to express to my teachers, managers at work, or even close friends that my home life was deeply affecting my quality of work and my ability to show up. At first it wasn't something I wanted to do, but I realized that even expressing that things weren't the easiest at home resulted in a lot of grace and endless support from others. Instead of getting more pressure from teachers, managers, or friends because I wasn't able to show up exactly the way they wanted me to, they helped me through it. It wasn't even about giving them intimate details of what was going on in my home, but simply by expressing that life was a little hard during certain times, I was given extra time in school to make up for assignments, more or less shifts depending on how stressful my week was at home, or simply my friends checking in on me on the days I felt alone. If you're finding it hard to handle things that are out of your control, I encourage you to reach out for extra support as you learn to navigate this phase of your life.

✦ **What I started to notice was that the home I lived in seemed to trigger me a lot due to being around people who weren't taking care of themselves, let alone the household.** I decided it would be best to stop trying to force myself to feel calm in an environment where it was complete chaos. So, no matter who I was living with or where I was, I always made sure to **create a safe space** in the comfort of my own room. Even if it was chaotic everywhere else in my home, my room was mine; *it was safe.* I always made sure to keep it clean, organized, and aesthetically pleasing. This helped me a lot with my mental health because when you wake up in a clean environment, sometimes it helps with your motivation to get up and continue on with your day. Now although having a clean and safe room helped me manage my anxiety, spending all my time in my room only did so much for me. This is where I started to take myself out of the chaotic environment by spending more time after class working on my assignments in the library, or even at a coffee shop. There were many days where instead of going home, I spent time relaxing and decompressing at my best friend's house. I even spent a lot of my mornings at the gym working on my fitness and listening to podcasts to help me stay focused. Whatever it was that I needed to continue to take on in my life, I learned different ways to help myself accomplish these tasks by taking distractions (at the time it was my chaotic, toxic environment and family issues) away from me by placing myself in healthier environments. Maybe your home life is not the toxic environment, but maybe it's your work environment or school. Whatever it is, think about ways you can remove yourself from certain situations that might not make you feel the best. Remember, work with what you have. It's understandable that you may not be able to remove yourself entirely from the environment, but could you go on a walk on your lunch break rather than sit around coworkers who gossip and complain? Could you sit at another table and eat your lunch while listening to an uplifting podcast or playlist instead of sitting around a group of friends who barely even act like you exist? Or maybe, instead of spending your weekends at home where you feel lonely or unsafe, you're reaching out to your aunt or grandma and setting up a plan to stay there on the weekends? I invite you to think about the little things you can do within your life to help clear out stress and anxiety that are created through forces outside of you.

✦ **Something that helped me through the roughest phases of my life, through my unhealthy home environments or the mental, physical, and financial issues I struggled with, was keeping my eye on my vision.** This is the thing: When life is feeling chaotic, when we've been given a deck of cards in which many of them haven't been favorable (such as low income, emotionally unavailable parents, health issues, etc.), we tend to lose sight of what it is we really desire within our lives. Although understandable, and not something to ignore, the more you direct your focus on the vision outside of the reality that is currently present, the more you move forward in that direction. For me, one of the most positive things that could have come out of my unhealthy addiction of Tumblr and social media in general was that I was exposed to so many different types of people living lives that I didn't have. And instead of thinking I could never have that life, I looked at those images as inspiration to work toward eventually getting that myself, and you should too. It took a few years for me to have a healthy relationship with the images I was looking at online, but once I implemented the previous tips, I was able to have a healthy relationship with the images I was using as inspiration. It is so important that we show ourselves that a better life is possible, or else we'll never feel the need to try and work toward a better life. Something I would do every season was create a vision board of all the things I wanted to accomplish and achieve for the next season to come. This really helped me when I would wake up and be faced with the reality that my home life was undesirable, because I had something to get up for. I got up to work toward the dream house, the dream career, the dream relationship. I no longer got up and waited for things to change, I got up and started to take action toward the vision I held for myself instead of waiting. *There's nothing to wait for.* Another thing that helped me all throughout my late teens and early twenties was watching some of my favorite people on YouTube living the life that I wanted. This at times would turn toxic if I wasn't careful with understanding that I didn't need to have their exact life to feel safe, but as I got older, I realized these people on the internet simply helped me expand my mind and showed me what was possible, so I continued to use them as motivation. I suggest that you find people who inspire you and motivate you, whether that be online or offline, and allow them to be the inspiration and "goals" for your dream life. I believe every successful person has practiced some sort of "holding their vision" before they've actually achieved the thing they wanted. This is what kept me sane and got me to where I'm at now in my life. I can honestly say I'm now living the life I envisioned on my dream board, and you can too.

This is the thing: There are going to be days where it's incredibly hard for you to redirect your focus, take yourself out of crappy environments, or believe it's possible for you to achieve your dream life the way it's been plastered all over your vision board, and that's okay. Quite frankly, I don't think you'd be able to call yourself human if you didn't have these doubts, fears, or stumbles on this journey of becoming the person of your dreams. All I want you to remember is that these undesirable situations, even when you don't believe it, in some way, somehow, are creating resilience so strong within you that once you get out of it, you will be floored to even comprehend how you navigated such times. On top of that, you will be immensely proud of the fact that you got through it. But there are a few things you're going to need to get good at when getting yourself through some of the hardest, most confusing phases of your life that will impact the version of you that you're trying to glow up into, which is your inner dialogue and the stories you tell yourself. This is what we will explore next.

Self-acceptance

" But it's how we treat ourselves on these days and respond to these circumstances that can bring us down a line of more undesirable outcomes or positive ones."

It's inevitable that we're going to come in contact with many ebbs and flows of life, such as people disappointing us, job opportunities not working out, breakups, bad body-image days, etc. But it's how we treat ourselves on these days and respond to these circumstances that can bring us down a line of more undesirable outcomes or positive ones. Something I've picked up on my glow-up journey was the ability to positively self-talk on the days that things don't go in my favor, or when I'm trying to work toward something I have yet to achieve. This is something I practice to this day, even after achieving so much success and healing in my life.

Positive self-talk is something most of us have not learned how to cultivate, yet it can be one of the most profound ways we transform our lives. The ability to be kind and loving to yourself on the days when you're not feeling the best, when you've made a mistake, or when you feel lost plays a huge role in your actions thereafter. Being okay with the fact that you had a bad day can create a lot of mental clarity for you to make the next best decision for yourself based out of self-love and compassion, versus deciding to be incredibly critical on yourself to the point where you want to take unloving action in the form of punishing yourself.

Let's take dieting for example. What many of us do when we've moved away from eating foods that we know are healthy for us, instead of firstly recognizing our patterns and exploring why we might have done that in the first place, we start feeling a lot of shame. We blame ourselves and try to restrict ourselves harder the next day, which creates an even bigger struggle to keep up with these standards and causes us to continue perpetuating the same cycle. When really, there's no need for us to shame ourselves, obsess over how much we've ruined our progress, and set harsher rules to make sure we don't do it again. If we can take a moment to self-reflect as to why we might have done an undesirable behavior, which we've gone through at the beginning of part two, and then learn to be okay with the fact that we've done that and lovingly pick ourselves back up, we end up moving in a direction that brings us closer to what we're trying to achieve in the first place, which is a state of love and happiness.

A practice that has been beneficial for me on my journey has been recognizing when I say hurtful and mean things to myself, whether that be pointing out imperfections or perceived mistakes I've made, and instead of criticizing and judging myself for these things, I simply practice the act of allowing myself to be okay with the fact that I look this way or I've done this thing. Sometimes I'll go as far as playing a scenario out, such as asking myself the question: What would it be like for a moment if I just allowed myself to accept that I don't look picture-perfect today? At first, it doesn't feel comfortable because that essentially means to my inner parts that I'm not going to be liked by others, but a follow-up question is, could I be okay with that? Could I be okay with knowing that not everyone will love me? Could I be okay with the fact that not everyone will accept me?

"Furthermore, the main reason why we aren't accepted and loved by absolutely everyone is because many people aren't even able to accept and love themselves."

What has helped me be okay with such circumstances is realizing that I'm not inherently wrong for looking or acting a certain way. It's okay that we humans are flawed and that we make mistakes or don't always have the answer. Furthermore, the main reason why we aren't accepted and loved by absolutely everyone is because many people aren't even able to accept and love themselves. On top of that we all desire, prioritize, and value different things in life. For example, if someone grew up on a farm and has taken care of horses their entire life and experiences a deep level of peace and happiness when they're around them, they will most likely value, invest in, and appreciate anything and everything to do with horses over someone who hasn't had that life experience. That doesn't mean that the person who doesn't have an interest in horses makes these horses invaluable, or unlovable; it's simply one person's preference over the other. On top of that, the most beautiful thing about reframing your mindset like this as you heal is that you start to recognize, let's say, the value of the horses, even if you wouldn't ever invest your time and money into such a thing. You start to see the beauty in others from afar, and how it would make so much sense as to how someone would value something so much more than you might, based on our individual preferences and life stories.

When you find yourself struggling with self-rejection, criticizing and judging yourself, remind yourself that you are safe and worthy of love and acceptance, even when you're not everyone's cup of tea. **Here's a few questions you can journal on during times of negative self-talk:**

Whose box am I trying to fit into?

Example: I've been taught that men like a certain body type, and I don't have that body type. So every time I fall off a diet, or don't look as good as the other girls when we go out, I feel like crap about myself, which makes me think I'll never be loved.

What would it feel like if I didn't fit into this box and was not accepted by these men?

Example: It would make me feel like I'm left out, not chosen, not picked, like I'll never find love.

_____

_____

_____

_____

_____

_____

_____

_____

_____

_____

_____

_____

_____

_____

_____

_____

_____

_____

_____

Now, if you had a young child (your own, a younger sibling, or family member) come up to you and tell you that they feel (whatever you wrote down), what would you say to them to help them feel better about themselves?

That is what you need to tell yourself. *That is positive self-talk.*

Becoming your own best friend, big sister, or nurturing mother or father that maybe you never had in times where you're feeling a lot of low self-worth is a practice that you will need to master throughout your journey, which will get easier over time. Once you learn to speak to yourself kindly, you're able to continue taking action toward the goals and dream life you have set forth for yourself. While speaking to ourselves lovingly will help us feel better about ourselves when it comes to our dream lives, it does require us to take action toward the things we want to accomplish. Sometimes, telling yourself you're amazing, beautiful, and deserving of everything you want in your life will only take you so far, because the next step above learning to speak positively to yourself is learning to instill confidence within yourself to actually take certain actions toward your goals. Most of the time, we have a specific story that we hold about our ability, or lack thereof, to take action. Let's explore that next.

The stories we tell ourselves

One thing I've been observing over the years within myself and in others is that we are so incredibly consumed by certain narratives and stories that we hold about ourselves and others in this world. On top of that, these stories directly correlate to our actions, and our actions are what get us the things we really want in our lives. So when we're not taking the actions we want to be taking, it's important to not only address the parts of us that might be self-sabotaging and why, but the stories and beliefs we hold which influence us to take certain actions or not. For instance, if you believe that the gym is hard, boring, and takes up too much of your time, you are naturally going to be inclined to never be excited about the gym, thus making it more difficult to commit. If you believe that you're not good at writing or speaking, you're naturally going to dread it when the time comes to do a project or prepare a speech. If you believe that all men disappoint you, cheat, or lie, you're naturally going to focus on finding evidence that supports that belief.

The thing is, we are constantly looking for cues of safety in our reality, and what we deem "safe" will depend on if it correlates to the beliefs we hold within our minds. If we've been believing that all men cheat, in order for us to feel safe and in control, we will subconsciously start to look for any evidence to confirm whatever bias we have. We will focus on any behavior that would align with the belief of "men always cheat." Your focus no longer is on a man's positive actions or how he's treated you; instead you keep a close eye on how many times he calls you (or doesn't) a day, in which you then create a story that would align to that belief system. So instead of assuming (because you have a better belief system about men) that he's genuinely busy with work, if you have a belief that all men are inherently cheaters, every time he's not in front of your face, you will assume he's out cheating on you.

Now, where we get stuck with changing certain narratives and belief systems is that sometimes we have actually been proven wrong, such as being cheated on. In fact, there's always some sort of situation at play which formed this negative story and belief about any area of our lives in the first place. So it's understandable why you would expect that these parts of your life would continue to play out the same way they always have. What's challenging about experiencing undesirable situations, such as unhealthy relationships or financial instability, is that we haven't really experienced anything else, so why would we believe in something outside of what we've only experienced? Or worse, we try to expect good things, but we struggle with believing deep down that things will be different. As challenging as it might be at first, it's going to be up to us to search, reframe, and look for healthier cues of safety within men, finances, friendships, etc. if we want a different outcome. We essentially need to tap more into our optimistic, positive, creator mindsets, instead of the victim mindset.

In order for me to start seeing changes in my life and take positive actions, I really needed to work on the stories I was telling myself about how life is and how people show up for me. I did this by witnessing how I was creating so much of my reality simply based on the assumption of bad things going wrong, even when they weren't. Many of my actions would perpetuate a negative belief I held about someone based on my past undesirable situations, and I would end up making the situation real because I started acting from this place of negative belief. I would start to falsely accuse, create fights, and lose my peace of mind by obsessing, checking, and stressing to the point where people and circumstances really had no other option but to conform to my narrative.

Again, this is not to deny that there aren't people in the world doing bad things, but let's take this as an example. If you had a positive belief system such as "the men I date and love show up for me" or that "I am deserving of someone who commits and honors a relationship the same way I do" because that's how you expect men to show up in your life, you tend to either catch on to when you might come in contact with a man who isn't acting in accordance to that belief system through picking up on very real red flags, or if you end up missing them, you stand in your worth enough to walk away instead of driving yourself crazy trying to change this person or stay in a unhealthy relationship. I know it can be harder said than done, but it's my opinion that the universe, god, whatever you want to believe in, sends you situations or people like this so that you can learn how to step into your worth, uplevel your life, and continue to experience what is best for you, rather than what's not.

I just don't believe we get handed certain unfavorable cards in life so that all we can do is suffer. Sure, there will be pain, but the suffering can be perpetuated by the person who is in pain a lot more than they think. I know that to be true because I've had moments where I would have rather blamed everyone else because realistically, they should be to blame, but I realized that I wasn't actually gaining my power back by blaming and complaining about how people were or were not showing up for me like they should have. I decided to step into the creator mindset versus the victim mindset and take my power back by asserting my boundaries, telling myself that I deserve better, and walking away from unhealthy situations. Instead, I trusted that I would get what I wanted with another person instead of waiting, forcing, and manipulating someone to change and love me. This got me the outcome I always desired and deserved in the first place.

Journal practice

If you want to see change within yourself and your life, it's going to be important to start to become aware of the stories you're telling yourself, and how you speak to yourself in these moments. Some things to ask when you find you're spiraling into a negative story are:

Is this story helping or hurting me?

_____

_____

_____

_____

_____

_____

_____

_____

_____

_____

_____

_____

Is this story based on what I've experienced in the past?

How could I reframe this story to allow myself to move forward in a positive way?

_____

_____

_____

_____

_____

_____

_____

_____

_____

_____

_____

_____

_____

_____

_____

_____

_____

_____

_____

_____

_____

_____

_____

_____

_____

_____

_____

_____

_____

_____

Where might I not be standing in my self-worth at this moment and what action do I know I need to take to get me closer to my desired outcome?

_____

_____

_____

_____

_____

_____

_____

_____

_____

_____

_____

_____

_____

_____

_____

_____

_____

_____

_____

_____

_____

_____

_____

_____

_____

_____

_____

_____

_____

_____

_____

_____

What are alternative ways I could reclaim the power that I might feel like I've lost?

_____

_____

_____

_____

_____

_____

_____

_____

_____

_____

Spending more time reframing your mindset by taking control over the stories you tell yourself, and choosing to believe in a more favorable story that benefits you in the moment by shifting your awareness to a positive outcome versus a negative one, will without a doubt change your life.

CHAPTER EIGHT

YOUR DECK
OF CARDS

" The true glow-up happens when you come *back home* to yourself. When you start becoming *more* like yourself, and *less* like them.**"**

After years of spending time going deeper into my story, meeting my inner parts, uncovering my shadows, and healing my wounds, I came to the conclusion that the way I thought I was going to glow up would be in the form of a new diet, a harder workout plan, or more followers on social media. Furthermore, I would achieve self-satisfaction through continuing to morph myself into becoming the Tumblr girl, win the validation from others, or finally convince someone that they should love me. But that wasn't the answer. That's not what did it for me. The secret, or the *reason* why I never felt "glowed up" was because this journey turned into a process of never-ending self-rejection. This journey became *how do I become less like myself, and more like them?* And my friend, my love, my younger self. The true glow-up happens when you come back home to yourself. When you start becoming more like yourself, and less like them.

You see, when we are born, we don't have the weight of the world on us. We aren't yet bombarded with negative narratives, how we should act or what we should look like. We don't struggle with stress-induced health issues, deep-rooted insecurities, and self-hate. It's only when we come into the world and get dealt a deck of cards that will unfortunately but inevitably start to bring us further and further away from our true authentic selves. But here's a mindset shift for you, which completely changed the way I look at this hard truth of life. Essentially, we get a deck of cards, and within those cards are things like certain parents and parenting styles, socioeconomic statuses, genes, environments we have to grow up in, and the list goes on. This all makes up a unique deck.

"So what will you choose?"

And what I learned on my glow-up journey was that the way I was perceiving my deck of cards was very skewed. I didn't understand that some of my cards didn't need to be traded or thrown away, such as my hair, my face, or my body type not being as popular as the rest. Realistically, many of my cards were unique and special, but I just didn't see the beauty in them yet. I also didn't understand that some of the unfavorable cards I had, such as toxic living environments, weren't completely out of my control. Even when I wasn't able to trade them in when I was young, I could change the way I perceived what was presented on such cards and I could find ways to work with them as part of my deck. But for you to be able to have flexibility with changing, upgrading, or working with the cards that were dealt to you, you will have to change the story you're telling yourself about your deck. If you think that all your cards are fixed, then they're fixed. If you believe you have the ability to change these cards, you will naturally start to look for opportunities and ways in which you can do so. If you think that the answer to all your problems is to trade or throw away every single card, which I thought I needed to do when I was sixteen, then you'll end up depleting your deck so much that you'll feel lost and empty. So what will you choose?

It's my belief there is always a reason for the cards that we were dealt and in fact, I look at life as if it's a journey of deeply understanding each card. What helped me truly transform my life was looking at every card as a lesson, a reason, a part of my blueprint here on earth. And although some of those cards were so unrecognizable as to what the lesson was at that moment, it didn't matter. Because it's not until you start going through the situation at hand, and start to reframe what this means in your life, that you will really be able to look at such cards as lessons, as reasons, as things that were meant to happen. Over time, you get better and better at seeing each life circumstance for what it is. And honestly, sometimes we go a lifetime without ever truly understanding the "why" behind a certain card, and that's okay too. If we can learn to work with these cards in the best way we can, that's simply all that matters. I think moving from a place of perfectionism and allowing yourself to be okay with not being okay, or being okay with not fully understanding or having everything exactly the way you think it needs to be, can really help you enjoy the present moment despite what cards are currently at play.

" Healing is not linear."

So my wish for you is to continue to take on this journey called life, despite its complexities. To continue to learn who the real you is. To continue to re-own all the cards that were dealt to you, that were always worthy to begin with. To continue to empower yourself to uplevel and change the cards that you know no longer serve you. For you to understand that healing is not linear, nor does it need to be. For you to understand it's okay that you don't have it figured out, that you don't fit into everyone's box, or that your life might not be the way you pictured yet. For you to continue showing up for your inner child the way it's always deserved. For you to no longer ignore, hate, and self-reject the parts of you that you never fully understood how to love and accept. For you to deeply understand that your glow-up is not about becoming the replica of someone you see online and in the media and instead, it's about becoming the most healthy, most healed, most confident version of *you*.

ABOUT THE AUTHOR

Elicia Goguen, creator of *The Glow Up Secrets* podcast, is passionate about inspiring and guiding her audience on their glow-up journeys, with a focus on internal healing and mental health and wellness. On her YouTube channel and podcast, she dives into topics like shadow work, inner-child healing, forming healthy habits, positive self-talk, and more. Her goal is to meet people where they are in their self-transformation journey and provide a safe space to grow with yourself and others. Her platform expands the traditional "glow-up" journey from something done for acceptance and acknowledgement from others to something you do for yourself regardless of the external validation.

After many years of struggling with her own mental and physical health due to her challenges with low self-esteem, stressful family dynamics, and chronic illness, she's learned how to heal and overcome situations that she once thought she had no control over. Using her wisdom, knowledge, and practices that she's picked up over the years, she's now cultivated a loyal community who look to her for advice on how to establish a self-loving and compassionate relationship with oneself, while navigating womanhood and adopting healthy lifestyle habits.

Join the online glow-up community and discover more content from Elicia:

Instagram @eliciagoguen / @theglowupsecretspodcast
YouTube @eliciagoguen / @theglowupsecretspodcast
TikTok @theglowupsecrets

Mango Publishing, established in 2014, publishes an eclectic list of books by diverse authors—both new and established voices—on topics ranging from business, personal growth, women's empowerment, LGBTQ studies, health, and spirituality to history, popular culture, time management, decluttering, lifestyle, mental wellness, aging, and sustainable living. We were named 2019 *and* 2020's #1 fastest growing independent publisher by *Publishers Weekly*. Our success is driven by our main goal, which is to publish high-quality books that will entertain readers as well as make a positive difference in their lives.

Our readers are our most important resource; we value your input, suggestions, and ideas. We'd love to hear from you—after all, we are publishing books for you!

Please stay in touch with us and follow us at:

Facebook: Mango Publishing

X: @MangoPublishing

Instagram: @MangoPublishing

LinkedIn: Mango Publishing

Pinterest: Mango Publishing

Newsletter: mangopublishinggroup.com/newsletter

Join us on Mango's journey to reinvent publishing, one book at a time.

SECRETS TO A
SUSTAINABLE
GLOW UP

Before and after photos are worth a thousand words, but do they tell the right story? Many women who find themselves at a low point in their lives and want to "glow up" are lured in by quick physical results, but Elicia Goguen of *The Glow Up Secrets* podcast is here to show you how to achieve a glow up that goes deeper than the physical and lasts a lifetime.

When starting the glow up journey, sometimes we approach it from a place of shame and low self-worth. *The Ultimate Glow Up Guide* peels back layers to motivate you from a place of self-love, and helps you create a vision that will keep you inspired and help you *enjoy* the process. If you are tired of repeating patterns, feeling less-than, and wondering when your life will truly begin, this book is for you.

IN *THE ULTIMATE GLOW UP GUIDE*, YOU WILL DISCOVER:

◊ Why you self-sabotage and how to finally break unhealthy cycles and limiting beliefs

◊ How to curb self-criticism and love yourself through a journey of self-transformation

◊ Ways to rebuild your self-worth and confidence in a society that breaks it down

◊ Reflections and journal practices to help you connect more deeply with your inner child

ISBN 978-1-6841-362-9
ISBN 978-1-68481-362-9
90000

9 781684 813629